# Child Day Care and Babysitting: The Complete Guide

# Child Day Care and Babysitting: The Complete Guide

Janice Jacobs

MURPHY & MOORE
www.murphy-moorepublishing.com

Child Day Care and Babysitting: The Complete Guide
Janice Jacobs
ISBN: 978-1-63987-105-6 (Hardback)



MURPHY & MOORE

Published by Murphy & Moore Publishing,
1 Rockefeller Plaza,
New York City, NY 10020, USA

**Cataloging-in-Publication Data**

Child day care and babysitting : the complete guide / Janice Jacobs.
p. cm.
Includes bibliographical references and index.
ISBN 978-1-63987-105-6
1. Child care services--Guidebooks. 2. Day care centers--Employees--Guidebooks.
3. Child care workers--Guidebooks. 4. Babysitting--Guidebooks. I. Jacobs, Janice.
HQ778.5 .C45 2021
362.712--dc23



For more information regarding Murphy & Moore Publishing and its products, please visit the publisher's website www.murphy-moorepublishing.com

# Table of Contents

# Preface

The services that involve the care of a child, from the age of six weeks to thirteen, is known as child day care. Babysitting is a temporary child care activity that requires the care for children at home. Commercial child care centers act as day cares and also provide basic education in reading, writing and arithmetic. In-house child care services are provided by professional nannies. This textbook unfolds the innovative aspects of child day care and babysitting, which will be crucial for the holistic understanding of the subject. It will serve as a valuable source of reference for those interested in this field.

Given below is the chapter wise description of the book:

Chapter 1- Providing care and supervision for children aged between six weeks to thirteen years is known as child care. Child care centers are facilities where children interact with each other, perform planned activities and play games. This chapter is an overview of the subject matter incorporating all the major aspects of child care.

Chapter 2- Parents leave their children in the charge of babysitters for a temporary period of time. It involves monitoring and caring for children, however, dependability and responsibility is part of this job. This is an introductory chapter which will introduce briefly all the significant aspects of babysitting with respect to child day care facilities.

Chapter 3- Child care centers provide places for social interaction among children. They can be provided with guidance to uphold good behavior. Providing a safe and nurturing environment is key for a child's cognitive and emotional development. Child care is best understood in confluence with the major topics listed in the following chapter.

Chapter 4- Day care centers can provide significant learning activities for the children to perform. Simple lessons can be taught and child participation can be rewarded with gifts and praise. The topics discussed in the chapter are of great importance to broaden the existing knowledge on child day care.

Chapter 5- Children require a different diet as compared to adults. Their nutritional needs and metabolism are unique. Hence, children at a day care must be provided with specially prepared, clean and hygienic food. The aspects elucidated in this chapter are of vital importance and provide a better understanding of food and nutrition at child day care.

Indeed, my job was extremely crucial and challenging as I had to ensure that every chapter is informative and structured in a student-friendly manner. I am thankful for the support provided by my family and colleagues during the completion of this book.

**Janice Jacobs**

# Understanding the Concept of Child Care

1

Providing care and supervision for children aged between six weeks to thirteen years is known as child care. Child care centers are facilities where children interact with each other, perform planned activities and play games. This chapter is an overview of the subject matter incorporating all the major aspects of child care.

## Child Care

Child care or childcare, child minding, daycare, or preschool is the caring for and supervision of a child or children, usually from age six weeks to age thirteen. Child care is the action or skill of looking after children by a day-care center, babysitter, or other providers. Child care can also include advanced learning environments that include early childhood education. Child care is a broad topic covering a wide spectrum of contexts, activities, social and cultural conventions, and institutions. The majority of child care institutions that are available require that child care providers have extensive training in first aid and are CPR certified. In addition, background checks, drug testing at all centers, and reference verification are normally a requirement. Child care can cost up to $15,000 for one year in the United States. The average annual cost of full-time care for an infant in center-based care ranges from $4,863 in Mississippi to $16,430 in Massachusetts.

Early child care is a very important and often overlooked component of child development. Child care providers are our children's first teachers, and therefore play an integral role in our systems of early childhood education. Quality care from a young age can have a huge impact on the future successes of children.

### Common Types

#### Licensed Home Day Care or Family Child Care

Licensed or unlicensed home day care is also referred to as family child care, or in home care. It refers to the care provided to a group of children in the home of a caregiver. State laws differ regarding rules for licensed versus unlicensed care. In Canada, most home daycares are unlicensed, and this is completely lawful. Licensing home daycares in Canada can help greatly with oversight, but at the cost of a large portion of the daycare provider's pay. Family child cares are small in size and provide families the same securities as a day care center, and also has the benefits of flexible hours, lower costs, accessibility, and cultural compatibility. Home-based providers can give more individualized care and therefore better meet the needs of working families. In addition, family care generally has a small ratio of children in care, allowing for more interaction between child and provider than would be had at a commercial care center. Family child care helps foster emotionally secure interpersonal relationships for everyone involved. The providers are able to communicate each day with parents on a personal level and share information about the development of the child. Providers care for multi-aged groups of children allowing children to remain with one caregiver for many years which helps children develop a sense of trust and security. Multi-aged settings allow children to learn from one another and allow siblings to stay together. Some family child care providers may offer parents more flexibility with hours of operation such as evening, weekend, overnight, and before and after school care.

## In-home Care

In home care is typically provided by nannies, au pairs, or friends and family. The child is watched inside their own home or the caregiver's home, reducing exposure to outside children and illnesses. Depending on the number of children in the home, the children utilizing in-home care enjoy the greatest amount of interaction with their caregiver, forming a close bond. There are no required licensing or background checks for in-home care, making parental vigilance essential in choosing an appropriate caregiver. Nanny and au pair services provide certified caregivers and the cost of in-home care is the highest of childcare options per child, though a household with many children may find this the most convenient and affordable option. Many nannies study towards childcare qualifications. This means they are trained to create a safe and stimulating environment for your child to enjoy and thrive in. Typically, au pairs or nannies provide more than routine child care, often assisting with daily household activities, including running errands, shopping, doing laundry, fixing meals, and cleaning house.

At the same time, a nanny or au pair is not always the best methods of childcare. Nanny care is the most expensive form of childcare. Recruiting a nanny can be costly when using a Nanny agency. Nanny agencies will, however, thoroughly check the applicants' references and run a criminal background check on the successful candidate. Weekly salaries for nannies are 2 to 3 times the cost of a week of daycare. It confines the child into a world of their own. It keeps them from interacting with other children a lot of the time. As mentioned the caregivers do not need licenses or background checks so there is no way of telling if a person is really qualified or has a criminal background (unless you live in a country where there is an option of obtaining home-based care through a government licensed and funded agency). These things should be taken in consideration when making a choice.

## Family Child Care

Family child care providers care for children in the providers' own home. The children are in a mixed age group with a low adult to child ratio. Care can be more personalized and individual. The hours may be more flexible and the provider may offer evening and weekend care for mothers who work second or third shift. The cost of care in a family child care is lower on average than that of a center.

Child care facilities in the US have the option of becoming accredited. This standard is set and regulated by an outside agency. In centers, NAEYC institutes it. For family child care providers, the National Association of Family Child Care Providers award the credentials.

## Center-based Care

Commercial care center also known as day cares are open for set hours, and provide a standardized and regulated system of care for children. Parents may choose from a commercial care center close to their work, and some companies offer care at their facilities. Active children may thrive in the educational activities provided by a quality commercial care center, but according to the National Center for Early Development and Learning, children from low quality centers may be significantly less advanced in terms of vocabulary and reading skills. Classes are usually largest in this type of care, ratios of children to adult caregivers will vary according to state licensing requirements. Some positives of commercial care are children gain independence, academic achievement, and socialization.

A childcare development center in South Carolina in the United States

Pre-school is often the term used to refer to child care centers that care primarily for 3 and 4-year old children. Preschool can be based in a center, family child care home or a public school. Head Start is a federally funded program for low income children ages 3 and 4 and their families. Similarly Early Head Start serves low income children birth to 3 years of age. The cost for the Head Start program is estimated at $9,000 per child. Head Start program provides federal grants directly to local agencies to provide comprehensive child development services for low-income children and families. Today, Head Start serves more than one million low-income children. Head Start programs aim to promote school readiness by enhancing the social and cognitive development of children through the provision of educational, health, nutritional, social and other services to enrolled children and families.

Infants may also be cared for in infant and child care centers. Resources for Infant Educators is a non-profit worldwide organization, founded by the late Magda Gerber, a specialist in Infant Care.

Another method of child care is for before and/or after school: the YMCA program. There are buses that bring the child to the location. YMCA website claims that its programs are staffed with people who understand the cognitive, physical, and social development of kids, the need children have to feel connected and supported in trying new things, and the caring and reinforcement parents and families need to help each other. The YMCA aims to enable preschoolers to experience early literacy and learn about their world, and school-age kids make friends, learn new skills, and do homework.

Most western countries also have compulsory education during which the great majority of children are at school starting from five or six years of age. The school will act *in loco parentis* meaning "in lieu of parent supervision".

In many locales, government is responsible for monitoring the quality of care. For instance, in Scotland Her Majesty's Inspectorate of Education is responsible for improving care and education for children from birth to eighteen. This is implemented by inspections carried out by HMIE itself or by other members of inspection and review teams. Inspection reports include feedback from staff and parents as well as the inspectors, aiming to provide parents and carers information to help them decide whether a particular child care setting is providing good quality child care and meeting government standards.

## Informal Care

Informal childcare is a variation of childcare that utilizes family members as a childcare system, for example grandparents and siblings. Informal childcare is an especially inexpensive form of childcare, and is utilized typically by those who are considered poor. Parents may need to utilize informal care for a variety of reasons. Typically informal childcare is necessary for families who do not have enough funds to finance placing their children in a more expensive child care facility. Those low income families are also more apt to work longer hours on an irregular and inflexible schedule, which ultimately makes using a childcare facility that has regular business hours unlikely. A study done by Roberta Iversen and Annie Armstrong explains that due to long and irregular working hours, sometimes including evenings and weekends, poor parents are more likely to utilize informal childcare.

Unlike those children who receive center-based or home based childcare, those children who receive informal childcare do not receive the same educational preparation and school readiness that center-based and home based children receive. In his book *Social Inequality and Social Stratification in US Society*, sociologist Christopher Doob finds that poor children are less likely to attend the center-based and home based childcare programs, which Doob finds that informal care thus results in the less developed school-related skills children need. Doob concludes that due to a lack of financial capital, poor families are thus subject to substandard amounts of human capital, which results in lower quality childcare programs, and ultimately leaves children at a cognitive disadvantage.

## Effects on Child Development

For many, the use of paid childcare is a matter of choice with arguments on both sides about whether this is beneficial or harmful to children. The parental decisions of leaving a child with someone and who that someone will be are two of the most difficult decisions in the lives of most parents. A parent fears for the safety and security of his/her child. They need to be able trust the person or facility they choose as a provider for childcare. Whether this person is family, friend, live in, center based, young, old, well educated, or barely trained, the parents want to feel comfortable leaving their children with them. To have trust in the caregiver, the parent wants to know what kind of effects the type of service they provide will have on the development of their child. The development of a child has many factors, but it is most directly influenced by the type and quality of care that is most regularly provided to the child.

Child development researcher, Lian Tong, analysed the results from a Haley and Stansbury experiment saying, "Parent responsiveness also facilitates cognitive, social, and emotional development and reduces negative emotions in infants." This study applies to more age groups than just infants. To sum that up, the amount of time that a parent or teacher is willing to spend teaching, listening to, playing with, and exploring with the child the more socially, emotionally, and educationally developed the child will become. Whether that child receives the majority of his or her care at a center or at its house, the biggest factor in deciding what will have the best effect on the child will be those willing to put in the time and effort it takes to properly develop a child's social, physical, and academic skills.

In discussing the numbers it is important to note that in 2001, more than one half of the children in the United States attended childcare facilities. This number has only increased as the number of working parents has increased. The increase in the amount of children that are required to have some sort of childcare service has made childcare facilities more necessary than they have ever been. The quality of childcare given by a facility is generally indicated by the center's cost of enrollment. If the center charges more for the service, it will generally provide better care to the children. Centers that charge more for their services can provide quality education, more current resources, and nicer facilities. These are all helpful when trying to educate a child academically. A higher standard for teachers, such as requiring a degree in early childhood education or a degree of the like, has shown to result in improved growth in the development of a child. The childcare system in France is a great example of this. They have two separate branches of early childhood childcare. These two separate branches are called crèche and école maternelle. Crèche is the program for infants and toddlers and école maternelle is part of the education system. They both require teacher to have a college degree and sometimes a specialized degree on top of that.

Whether at an expensive facility or relatively inexpensive, children who attend daycare facilities tend to develop social skills more quickly than children of the same age group that are reared at home. They communicate better with children of the same age and often try harder to communicate with those that are younger than them, by using patience and taking different approaches at presenting the data. Surprisingly, a study done by Erik Dearing, has proven that negative social behavioral patterns are not directly connected to daycare. By studying a large selection of children from the Norwegian childcare system he concluded that the amount of hours a child spends at a daycare and their behavior have no dependent relations. Though in America, Children who attend childcare systems have a higher risk of externalizing the symptoms of negative social behavior, exhibiting these traits can directly correlate with their time spent in the center.

There are links between the income, education, and importance of consistency and the well being of the child, to the parents, and the development of their child. Higher educated parents place more importance on the education of their children than the parents who do not have a college degree or have not graduated from high school. Likewise, parents who have a higher income level are more willing to part with their money to purchase a private tutor or nanny to assist the parent in the education of their child. They also tend to stress the importance of being socially inept. The first few years of a child's life are important to form a basis for good education, morality, self-discipline and social integration. Consistency of approach, skills and qualifications of caregivers have been shown in many studies to improve the chances of a child reaching his or her full potential. Child care in much of western society is currently in crisis: there are not enough daycare spots, the cost for most parents is beyond their means, and child care staff are grossly underpaid. Starting wages for Early Childcare Educators start at $11 or $12, causing a high turnover rate, and decreases the likelihood of potentially safe, effective, and loving child care providers from even entering the field. According to a survey done by HiMama, 68% of for-profit child care organizations ranked 'Labor' as their top risk and 65% ranked 'Talent and Recruitment' as their top priority for 2017.

## Health Issues

### Childcare Infection

Childcare infection is the spread of infection during childcare, typically because of contact among children in daycare or school. This happens when groups of children meet in a childcare environment, and there any individual with an infectious disease may spread it to the entire group. Commonly spread diseases include influenza-like illness and enteric illnesses, such as diarrhea among babies using diapers. Illnesses and diseases may also include ring-worm, head lice, and hand, feet, mouth disease. It is uncertain how these diseases spread, but hand washing reduces some risk of transmission and increasing hygiene in other ways also reduces risk of infection.

### Value of Unpaid Childcare

Parents and mothers especially spend a significant amount of time raising their children. These mothers nurture and develop their children into being functional members of society- hard work that is not motivated by monetary gain. For centuries it has been assumed that women will stay home and take care of the children while their husbands go out and work. In most cases, the husbands get all the credit for providing for the family. However, their homemaker wives deserve just as much credit for their care work. Caregivers do not receive monetary compensation and they must pay a 'care-penalty.

A care-penalty is the price one pays for doing care work for a family member. Care giving demands a lot out of an individual, and as a result there is a high opportunity cost. The opportunity cost can relate to both time and money. Instead of taking care of a family member, a caregiver could spend time working or performing more leisure activities. Care penalties are not strictly related to childcare- they can also refer to taking care of a sick family member, babysitting a younger sibling, or taking an elderly family member to his/her doctor's appointments.

Studies have been done to get an annual salary estimate for a female caregiver. One survey suggested that the value of a mother's work, if she were paid the average wage for each task she performs in running the household and caring for her children, is $117,867 per year. The reason for the high salary is because mothers typically perform about 10 different job functions throughout the week. Some of these job functions are poorly paid, including cleaning, driving, caring for children, and washing laundry, but others, especially financial and managerial tasks that the survey equated with being the Chief Executive Officer of a company, are highly paid. Neither a nanny nor a housekeeper makes nearly as much money, and almost all of these tasks except direct child care also have to be done by non-parents.

It is important to assess the value of caregivers because they are what truly make society function, and often their work is under-appreciated. They prepare the next generation for school, work, and decision-making. A child's entire future largely depends on how he/she was nurtured. Not only does the child depend on this care, but the schools and employers also depend on the childcare. The government also benefits because these children will eventually become taxpayers, congressmen, and voters. Eventually, they will be the ones running the country. The value of unpaid childcare is also an important figure in various legal entities. Expert witnesses (most often economists) are occasionally brought into court cases to give estimates on the value of unpaid labor. By giving estimation, the plaintiff or defendant can be fairly compensated for their labor.

## Learning Stories

Learning Stories are documents that are used by Carers and educators in childcare settings. They use a story- telling format instead of a traditional 'observation' report to document the different ways that young children learn, and capture the moment in greater detail and provide parents with a greater insight into the events that occur in their child's time in childcare.

## What they Include

- Story of the child's progress
- Pictures of the experiences (Optional)
- The child's strengths, interests and needs
- Space for parent feedback

Learning stories originate from New Zealand as they use a learning model in their curriculum called "Te Whaariki". It highlights children's learning outcomes as 'disposition' which are "situated learning strategies plus motivation-participation repertoires from which a learner recognize, selects, edits, responds to, resists, searches for and constructs learning opportunities"

# How to open a Child Care Business

Operating a child-care business is a great way to earn a living if you enjoy working with children. Generally speaking, there are two main ways to run a child-care business. If you want to care for a large amount of children, your best option is to start a center-based business. Those with children of their own—or who want to work from home—may want to consider a home-based, or family, child-care center. Whichever form you choose, you will want to understand how to properly set up your business.

## Part 1

## Developing a Business Plan

1. Assess the need for child care in your community. Before you decide to open a business that provides child-care services, your first step should be to research the market for that service in

your community. There are several ways you can obtain this information, but perhaps the best way to do this is to talk directly to local parents to determine the specific child-care needs of the community in which you want to do business. Try some of the following:

- Interview several families and ask the parents what type of child care they could benefit from, and the extent to which this type of service is already provided by local businesses.
- Look at census data for your community, including the number of working families with children of an appropriate age, the number of recent marriages, and the income distribution of those families. You can find this information from a number of sources, including the U.S. Census Bureau or your local municipal government office.

2. Identify existing child-care businesses. Your next step should be to determine who your potential competitors might be. If there are a number of businesses in your area offering a certain type of child care, it would be best for you to distinguish yourself by serving a need yet unmet in your community. Consider some of the following when evaluating your potential competitors:

- What age groups are already being served?
- What are the hours of the other businesses?
- What types of child-care services are already on offer in your community?
- How many of these types of businesses already exist in your community?

3. Decide whether you will operate a home-based or center-based child-care business. While

the specific types of child care you may decide to offer are numerous, there are basically two forms of child-care businesses: (1) a business run out of your home or (2) a business run at an independent location. Which type of child-care business you would like to run will determine what you will need to account for in your budget and what legal requirements with which you will have to comply.

- When making this decision, consider that home-based child-care businesses generally have fewer expenses and lower overhead, have more flexible hours, and are more convenient for you and, likely, the parents whose needs you will be serving. The legal requirements to operate a home-based child-care business are also generally less strict than those for a center-based child-care business.
- On the other hand, a center-based business—while probably more expensive to establish and operate—will provide greater space so you can expand your business and earn greater revenue.

4. Decide what kind of child-care business you want to operate. After deciding whether you wish to operate your child-care business at home or in an independent facility, the next step is to decide what type of child care you would like to offer. Perhaps the best way to start making this decision is to examine your motivations for going into the child-care business. By considering why you want to get into this type of business in the first place, you can better understand what exactly you want to offer your community.

- Do you want to offer care based around a particular faith?
- Do you want to offer a learning environment focused on building or reinforcing skills?
- Do you want to offer a space for children to come and play?
- Deciding what type of service you will offer up front will not only allow you to build the business you want, but it will also allow you to budget for the things you might need to run such a center effectively (educational materials, toys, etc.).

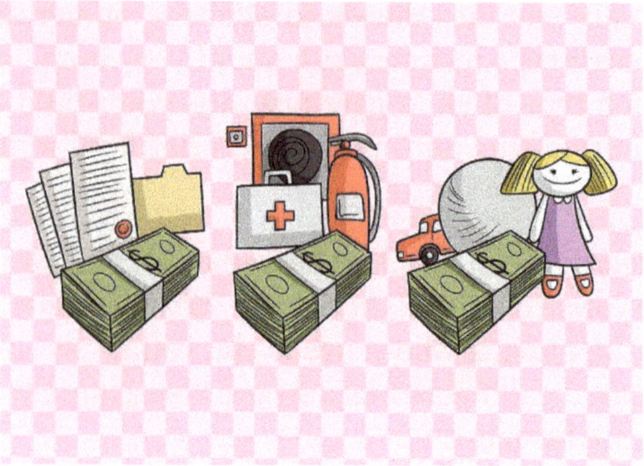

5. Make a budget. One of the most important things you can do when preparing to start a business is to make a budget. Doing so will help you plan for the future of your business, and ensure that it has the opportunity to succeed based on the funding you have available to you. You should consider start-up expenses, annual expenses, and monthly operating expenses. When making your budget, consider the following types of expenditures:

- Licensing, inspection, and insurance fees.
- Medical testing and clearance.
- Safety devices (e.g., smoke alarms, fire extinguishers, carbon-monoxide detectors, first-aid kits, child-proofing supplies, etc.).
- Food, toys, and equipment for your planned activities.
- Wages for prospective employees.
- Advertising/legal/professional-service fees.
- Rent, mortgage, and utility fees.

6. Choose a name for your business. One of the more important steps in the process is choosing a name for your business, because that is what will represent your services to the outside world. Your name should be catchy, easy to remember, and should indicate the type of service you will be providing.

- You will need to check with the secretary of state's office for your state to ensure that your proposed name does not conflict with any other name currently on record with the secretary of state.

7. Choose a type of business entity. There are several different types of legal structures for your potential business, each with its own benefits and drawbacks. For instance, if you operate as a sole proprietor, you will have likely have an easier time filing your taxes. However, if you operate as a corporation or a limited-liability company, you will be able to limit your liability for anything that happens while you operate your business to the funds that you placed in your business (i.e., you will not be personally liable).

- You should strongly consider speaking with a local attorney experienced in business formation/structure in order to get a good understanding of the different types of structures available to you before you choose one.

## Part 2

### Setting up your Child-Care Business

1. Contact your local country municipality. Once you have a business plan in place and are ready to actually start setting up your business, your first step should be to contact your local government to determine what legal requirements with which you must comply in order to properly run a child-care business in your county. You should ask this office:

- What sort of business license you need to operate your business, and how to obtain this license.
- What sort of building codes you must meet.
- What sort of occupancy laws are in effect in your county (i.e., how many children will you be able to take care of legally?).
- You can also contact your local child-care agency (an arm of state government) by typing in your zip code on this website and clicking "search for your local agency."

2. Select a location. If you plan to operate your child-care business out of your home, then this step is already complete. If you plan to open a separate facility, however, you will need to choose one that is in a good location that you can afford based on your budget. You will also need to consider, depending on your available funding, whether you will buy or rent this space. If you are looking for a location outside of your home, consider the following factors when making your selection:

- Is the location convenient for parents?
- Does public transportation serve your proposed location?
- Is the area safe?
- Is the space adequate for the business you intend to run there?
- Does it have adequate kitchen/bathroom facilities/fixtures?

3. Contact your county's zoning office. You will have to make sure that your proposed location

complies with local zoning laws. To do this, contact your county's zoning office and inquire as to whether your proposed location is properly zoned for child care.

4. Prepare your facility for inspection. This should consist of tasks like installing cabinet locks, setting up changing tables if you are servicing infants and/or toddlers, putting up smoke detectors, and inserting electrical outlet covers. You may also need to post an emergency evacuation plan.

- If you do not pass the first time, you will likely be given an opportunity to correct the errors and arrange to be inspected again.

5. Schedule necessary inspections. Depending on your jurisdiction, you will likely have to obtain a series of inspections to ensure that your proposed location complies with local health and safety laws. You may have to schedule some or all of the following:

- A fire-safety inspection.
- A health inspection.
- An environmental health inspection.

6. Obtain necessary licenses. In the vast majority of cases, you will have to apply for and be granted the proper licensing in order to care for children. The type of licensing you will need will depend on your jurisdiction. Your local municipal government office should be able to tell you what licenses you will need to obtain in order to run your child-care business. Your state's licensing office should also be able to provide you with an overview of the licensing requirements applicable to you, which you should read carefully. This process will likely involve some or all of the following:

- Attending an orientation session where you will learn about state and local requirements for operating your business and complying with applicable state law.
- Filling out a licensing application.
- Paying a licensing fee.
- Working with the licensing agency as it reviews your business plan, inspects your facility, and completes the licensing process.
- Taking classes focused on CPR, first-aid, and the like.
- Undergoing a background check (and fingerprinting) for you and any prospective employees.
- Undergoing medical testing/immunizations for you and any prospective employees.

7. Obtain necessary insurance. Generally speaking, you will also have to obtain liability insurance for your child-care business. You will be taking care of other people's children and, as such, you

should provide the best care and attention possible. It will provide peace of mind to prospective clients and to you that your business is protected financially for any situation that might arise.

- Your local municipal government office should be able to tell you which types of insurance are required based on the type of child-care business you intend to start.

8. Comply with appropriate tax laws. Depending on the type of legal structure you selected for your business, you will have to contend with differing tax obligations, including the forms you will use and the types of taxes you must pay.

- As with choosing a legal structure for your business, tax law is quite complex and you should strongly consider enlisting a tax specialist to ensure you are paying taxes properly and complying with applicable law.

9. Purchase necessary equipment. The type of child-care business you want to operate will largely dictate what kinds of equipment and/or materials you will need to obtain in order to run your business successfully. Children of different ages have different needs and interests, and the type of activities you will offer will obviously require different equipment and supplies to operate effectively. You will likely need to acquire some or all of the following:

- Child-sized furniture (tables, chairs, desks, etc.).
- Arts and crafts materials (pencils, crayons, paper, safety scissors, etc.).
- Toys (games, puzzles, dolls, action figures, Legos, building blocks, etc.).
- Children's books.

- Healthy, nutritious snacks/meals.
- Storage containers for personal belongings, hangers for coats, etc.

10. Hire employees. Depending on the size of child-care business you wish to operate, you may need to hire additional staff to help you with the daily operation of your facility. Be careful when selecting your staff, as they will be working in close contact with the children in your care and, as the employer, you will be responsible for their conduct on the job. When evaluating a potential candidate, keep the following in mind:

- Try to find candidates that have previous employment experience working with children (e.g., babysitters, teachers, camp counselors, etc.).
- Educational credentials are important as well. Look for potential hires who have received academic training in child care, child education, child development, or a similar field.
- While not necessarily a legal requirement in all jurisdictions, you should also consider if a potential hire has any relevant certifications, like CPR or first-aid training.
- Depending on the laws of your particular state, you will also likely need to ensure your employees have passed certain background checks, such as state and federal criminal-record-history checks or child-abuse checks.

## Part 3

### Running your Child-care Business

1. Develop a marketing strategy. Any successful business depends on a sound marketing strategy that makes the community aware of the great services you will offer. Before you begin advertising, try taking some time and thinking about the information you want to convey. Consider the following:

- Think about how you will describe the particular service you plan to offer. How is it different/better than what is already out there? What ages do you serve? What will your hours be?
- Think about the price you will charge, based on your previous market research, so that you can be competitive with other child-care businesses in the area.
- Think about the advantages your location offers (great parking, safe, convenient, etc.).
- If you have staff, think about how to market them as well. What qualifications/certifications/specialities do they bring to your business?

2. Advertise. You should begin advertising about three months before your child-care business is set to open. If you have the funds, newspaper, radio, and television ads will probably give you the greatest exposure, but these advertising formats do not come cheaply. Consider some of the following, less expensive options as well, even if you can afford more conventional advertising:

- Word of mouth.
- Posting fliers/posters in public spaces in your community (be sure to get permission from the owner of the property/building you plan to put your fliers on first, though!).
- Distributing brochures/business cards at libraries, church meetings, PTA meetings, neighborhood get-togethers, etc.
- Placing an ad in the classified section of a local paper.

3. Develop a daily schedule. You will also need to decide what, if any, your daily activities will be. Some child-care business offer little structure—they provide supervision and make toys/games/food available for the children to use, but have no set routine or schedule. Others take a more

planned approach, with time set aside for playing, learning, napping, etc., based on the ages of the children being cared for. Take some time and think about what you will offer the children for whom you will be caring, and what sort of schedule you will offer.

- If you are unsure of how to begin, try asking parents in your area what they would like a child-care facility to offer or perhaps how they structure their child's time at home.

## How to make your Day Care more Eco Friendly

Many families have made major and minor adjustments to their lifestyles to create a greener, more eco-friendly household. Many parents feel more comfortable leaving their children with caregivers that have the same values. Eco-friendly day cares are becoming popular as more people reach out to create a healthier world. Small changes can help make your day care more eco-friendly.

### Method 1

#### Eco-Friendly Cleaning

1. Find a way to make your day care germ-free through eco-friendly cleaning. Refrain from using chemicals as much as possible.

- Use alternatives to cleaning with chlorine bleach. Peroxide-based bleach, quaternary ammonia, and borax are all safer options for the environment and the children.
- One multi-purpose green cleaner is ionized acidic water from a water ionizer. When made at 2.7 pH, ionized acidic water has been lab tested and proven to kill E.Coli and staph bacteria on contact. It is safe and effective on plastic toys, countertops, floors, glass, toilets, door handles and even on the skin so no gloves or masks are needed. You can make it for pennies on the gallon by hooking a water ionizer up to your tap and filling a plastic spray bottle with it.
- Refrain from buying aerosol spray cans. Instead, create your own air fresheners using essential oils and baking soda.
- Create your own cleansing products from ingredients you can trust rather than purchasing cleaners full of chemicals.

- Mix ingredients such as vinegar, borax, mild detergent, antibacterial essential oil and water to make products such as window cleaner, mold and mildew remover, carpet spot cleaner and all-purpose cleaner.

## Method 2

### Eco-Friendly and Eco-Healthy Plastics

1. Use caution when buying or using plastic materials, including toys. Certain plastics have a negative effect on health.

- Stay away from plastics that contain the recycling codes 3 (PVC), 6 (PS) and 7 (other).
- Only buy sippy cups and bottles that are "BPA-free." These are safer for children.
- Do not use plastic containers to heat foods in a microwave.
- Preserve food with PVS-free plastic wrap.
- Look for toys that say naphthalene-free or PVC-free on the labeling.
- Throw away any plastic spoons, plates, sippy cups or bottles that have scratches on them.

## Method 3

### Eco-Friendly Pesticides

1. Consider Integrated Pest Management (IPM), which is safer for the children and the environment. Use pesticides only when necessary and no other options are available.

- Clean up any food or drink spills or crumbs as soon as they occur so they do not attract pests.
- Fill in cracks and holes with expandable foam or caulking to prevent pests from entering through them.
- Use a garbage can with a lid and take the trash out daily.
- Store food in sealed containers. Pests need food and water. Do not leave either out for their taking.

## Method 4

### Eco-Friendly Lessons

1. Begin to teach children about recycling and taking care of the environment.

- Model eco-friendly habits by using recycled supplies for art projects. Purchase recycled paper.
- Plant a garden with the children. Harvest the crops and enjoy a healthy snack.
- Take nature hikes or walk around the premises and discuss how various plants and animals help the environment.

## Method 5

### Eco-Friendly Snacks

1. Buy organically grown fruits, vegetables, and snack foods. Teaching children to enjoy these foods at an early age is healthier for the child and better for the environment.

# How to become a Certified Daycare Provider

For someone who absolutely loves kids, being a certified daycare provider would not even feel like a job. However, the process of becoming certified can take some time and varies from state to state, so exercising your patience is a must. Once you've attained your goal of becoming certified though, you'll find the whole process to be a very rewarding experience.

## Steps

1. Get in contact with the department of child services for your state to determine the laws and requirements within your locality. Rules and regulations differ from state to state, so make sure that you are aware of the ones applicable to you. For instance, there are some states which may not even require a license anymore, depending on the circumstances.

2. Go through the paperwork that the department of child services sends through mail. Make sure that everything is filled out completely, honestly, and to the best of your ability. When you are done, return the completed documents to the department of child services in your state through mail as well.

3. Check with your caseworker on the classes or trainings you are required to take for your certification. A caseworker will be assigned by the department of child services to help you. The caseworker will run a background check on you, and will make sure that you are fit to become a certified daycare provider. For instance, some states may require you to attend a child CPR (cardiopulmonary resuscitation) training, but even if your state does not, it is still a very important and useful skill to have. Aside from this, there are other trainings that your state might require you to take, so make sure to accomplish this first.

4. Take some online classes while waiting on your license. Although taking these courses are not required, they are still highly encouraged, as they provide a good amount of information on the topics that you should be aware of as a daycare provider. There are helpful classes for topics such as activities, meals, rules, and sanitation.

5. Use the time to complete any other requirements that your state might have, while you are waiting for the approval of the license. The time it takes to get licensed differs from state to state, so it would be best to ask your local child services department for the typical processing time in your locality.

# An Overview of Babysitting

2

Parents leave their children in the charge of babysitters for a temporary period of time. It involves monitoring and caring for children, however, dependability and responsibility is part of this job. This is an introductory chapter which will introduce briefly all the significant aspects of babysitting with respect to child day care facilities.

## How to Babysit

Babysitting a young child, whether a sibling or a next door neighbor, requires training, patience, and understanding. Oftentimes a rite of passage for young teenagers, babysitting can seem daunting without proper preparation. With a bit of planning and coordination, babysitting can be both enjoyable and lucrative.

### Part 1

### Becoming a Babysitter

1. Attend a childcare or babysitting class. In some places it is necessary to be licensed or certified before babysitting, either way it is helpful to know basic child-care responsibilities and techniques. Look for child-care, CPR, and first-aid classes in your area so that you are well-prepared and qualified for your first babysitting job. These can often be found at Red Cross, YMCA, and other community centers. You can also read books that cover the subject and answer many common questions about how to handle infants and children in many of the common situations.

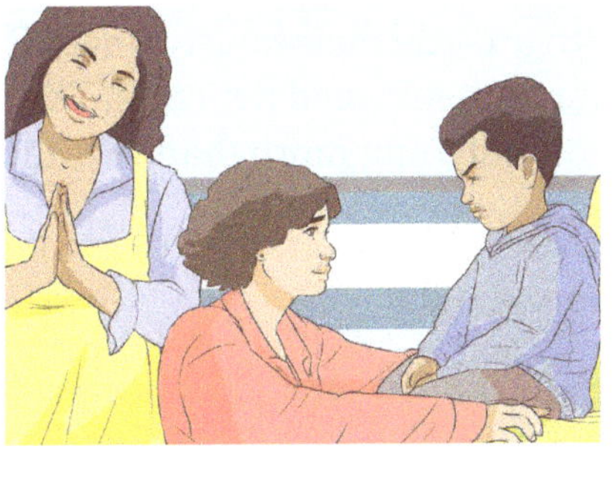

2. Be a mother's helper. Being in a home while a parent is there will give you a chance to practice

and gain experience you can advertise. Helping out with your own siblings is excellent practice, too.

3. Set up a schedule. As a babysitter, you are likely working for yourself (rather than a company) and therefore, have to make and maintain your own schedule. Although it may seem old-fashioned, fill out a calendar with all your free days and times, so that when a parent calls to schedule you for babysitting you know exactly when you are available.

- Creating a color-coding system may be helpful in organizing your 'busy' days on the calendar.
- Update your schedule frequently so that you don't accidentally double-book yourself.

4. Decide upon a rate of pay. Although some parents have a specific rate in mind when they hire a babysitter, many rely on the sitter to provide their hourly wage. There are two options for selecting a rate: being paid a flat rate per hour, or being paid per child. The former is better for small families while the latter is best if you plan on watching more than two children at once.

- Flat rate hourly wages typically range from $7-$12 per hour, but can be significantly more or less depending on the household.
- Per child wages range from $4-$6 per child, per hour. However, to get a better idea of the competition and to see what is suitable for the conditions, get an overview of what others in your area are charging for a family the size of the family you are sitting for.

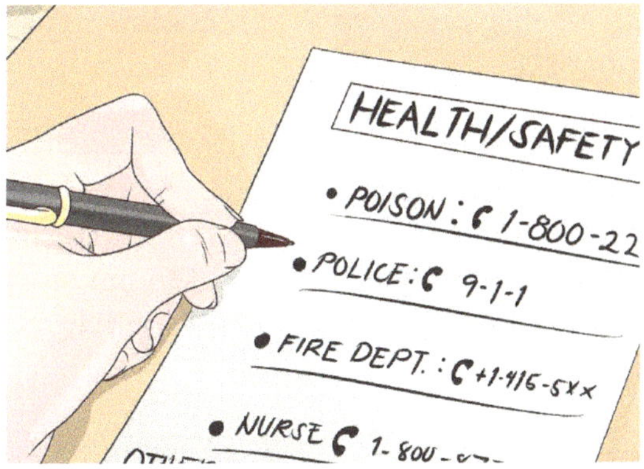


5. Create a list of health/safety information. You will also need personalized information for each child (such as allergy information), but you should have one generalized list of "worst-case-scenario" phone numbers. You may want to include:

- Poison control
- Police station
- Fire department
- Nurse hotline
- A trusted person who has had children (like an aunt or parent) to contact in case of a minor case of confusion
- Any other relevant numbers

6. Market yourself. If you're new to babysitting, you'll need to let people know you're interested. Word of mouth is often the easiest way to land a job. Talk to your neighbors, people from your church, or families at your school who have young kids. Ask friends who are babysitters if they know of any openings. If you have an older sibling who is moving on to another job, contact their clients.

- It's always best to babysit for someone you know or someone you've heard about from a friend. If you're new to babysitting, you may choose to *only* babysit for those you know.
- If word of mouth doesn't work, consider advertising in your neighborhood. You can put flyers in people's doors or send out an email if your neighborhood provides a list of residents.

If you decide to advertise, check with your parents first. They need to know anytime you put out personal information.

- Put together a résumé outlining any specific skills and experience you can offer. For example, if you took a babysitting course, put it on your résumé. List any experience you have had caring for kids — even if it's younger brothers, sisters, or cousins. Have you taken a first-aid course in school? Do you drive? These are all things to put on your résumé. Before you start, you also need to know how often or how much you want to work and what you plan to charge.

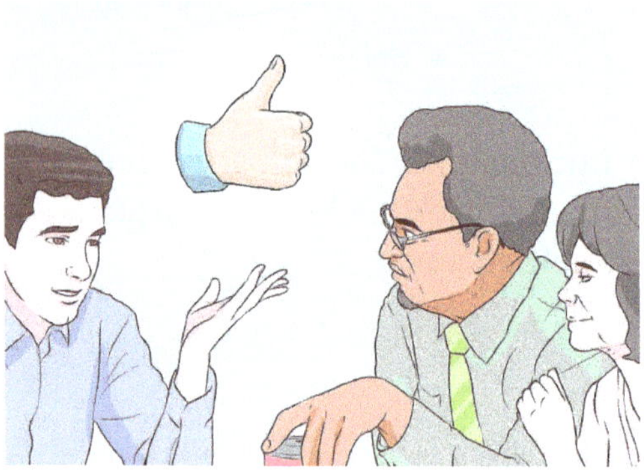

7. Know what to do when being interviewed. It's hard enough to find parents who are looking for babysitters. The next step - perhaps the hardest - is to make yourself seem worthy of the job. It's easier said than done. Now it's time to set up interviews so you can get to know the parents and their children.

- Just as you'll be finding out if the job sounds good, the parents will be looking to learn as much as possible about you. Tell them about yourself, your family, your school, and why you want to babysit.
- Be prepared with a list of questions so you know what's expected of you. Write them down so you don't forget to ask anything. The answers you get to questions like these will help you decide if it's the right job for you.
- If you've interviewed the family and met the kids but still want to learn more, suggest another visit so you can spend more time with the kids. Most parents will be happy that you want to find out as much as you can.

8. Know your comfort zone and its limits. Before you go, know what you're comfortable with and

what you're not. You need to feel in control. If you're unsure about a job, it's better to wait for the next one. Your safety is as important as the safety of the kids you'll be watching. If this is a first babysitting job, make sure you feel comfortable about the family. Trust your instincts, and don't feel like you have to accept the job on the spot. Tell the family you need to talk it over with your parents before committing to the job. When you know what you want and what to expect, babysitting is a better experience for both you and the kids.

- If you don't feel like you have the skills to look after a newborn, don't take the job.
- If you're allergic to certain animals, you may need to turn down a job if the family has pets.

9. Ask yourself these questions before you decide to take the leap.

- Do you enjoy spending time with children?
- Are you prepared to take care of kids?
- Do you have an awareness of young children's needs?
- Have you taken a babysitting course?
- Do you have experience taking care of younger siblings or relatives?
- What can you offer to the kids and their families?
- Do you want to babysit occasionally or find a regular babysitting position?
- If income is a concern, will the hours and payment meet your needs?
- How many kids will you be taking care of?
- What are their ages? The amount of care needed differs with age.
- Do the kids have any special needs? Special diets?
- Does the family have pets? A pool?
- What are the hours you're expected to work?

- What are you allowed to do in the home (e.g., use their computer, help yourself to food and snacks or bring your own)?
- If you have your license, are you expected to drive the kids?

## Part 2

### Preparing for the Job

1. Get the parents' and child's information. When you arrive on site for the job, start by getting all the information about the parents' whereabouts for when they leave. Write down their full names and phone numbers, the address(es) of their destination(s), and their estimated time of arrival back at the house, and an emergency contact. Also take down any information on the child, such as allergies (or other health information). This list will need to be longer and more detailed for longer time periods.

- Have the parents show you the location of first aid supplies and medications.
- Get a list of medications that each child may need to take, or is able to take in case of injury or illness (such as Tylenol for growing pains or a headache).
- Write down the child/children's schedule. Most families have a general (or sometimes more specific) timetable of events in a child's day. This typically includes meal times, the times for certain chores/homework periods, and bedtime. Getting this written down in advance will mean that the child (if they're older) won't be able to pull the wool over your eyes once their parents are gone.

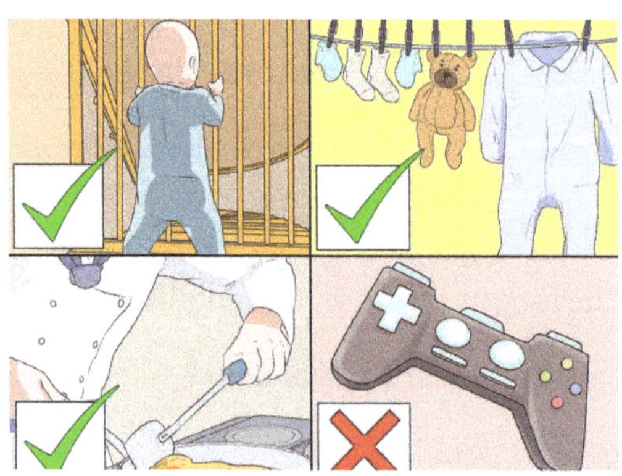

2. Find out what activities are allowed. Each household you work in will be slightly different, and

it is important to find out what activities are allowed in each. Ask about television/video game/computer time, when/where the child may be allowed to play outside, if their friends are allowed over, and any areas of the house that may be off-limits. These rules may vary from child to child in the same household depending on age, so be sure to specify.

3. Set up a menu for your time there. Depending on how long you'll be babysitting, you may have to feed the child/children a meal or two. Ask the parents about what foods they prefer you cook and serve, and what foods are appropriate for snack time. Clarify about any foods that aren't allowed; these are typically candy and dessert-related goodies that the kids might ask for when their parents aren't supervising.

4. Find out what appropriate punishments are used, when the child misbehaves. It is fairly likely that at some point in time, a child you are watching will misbehave. Rather than guessing and either punishing them too little or too much, ask the parents what they typically do for small misbehaviors. Many times this includes having privileges revoked or being put on 'time-out'. A parent could also say that you are not to punish them, and instead should report all misbehaviors to them.

# Part 3

## Watching the Kids

1. Spend time getting to know the kids. Babysitting is as much a job as it is an opportunity to enjoy the company of children. The kids will be more receptive to you and your rules if they like you, and they'll grow to like you faster if you try to develop a relationship with them. Talk with them, ask them questions, and joke around in order to develop a good relationship.

2. Join in with their play time activities. Although your job is to watch over the children, you should be interacting with them as much as possible by playing with them. Play will vary based on their ages; if you're watching an infant you may be doing nothing more than making faces and holding up toys. Get creative with the things you come up with for the children to do to keep them interested and out of trouble. Make-believe games are great fun.

- Be an entertainer. Parents love babysitters who help kids have fun and learn while still reinforcing rules and keeping discipline. Ask kids to show you their favorite toys. Find out from parents and other babysitters what games kids of different ages like to play. Get the kids outdoors if you can.
- Playing with toys, board games, and activity-based games are all good options for older children. Ask what their favorite thing to do is. You can also bring a few of your favorite games and toys from when you were their age.
- Monopoly
- Life

- Candyland
- Uno
- Card games

3. Tell stories. Kids like stories, and they'll be impressed by even the worst storytellers. Come equipped with obscure fairy tales they probably haven't heard, like "The Shoemaker and the Elves" or "The Twelve Dancing Princesses." You can even use stories as rewards.

4. Come up with fun projects. If you're spending a long time watching the children, you can do projects together that are enjoyable for everyone. Consider doing an arts and crafts project or cooking/baking a new recipe (or an old favorite) together. Boxed mixes of brownies, cookies, and cakes taste delicious. Having a finished product will feel productive, pass the time, and give the kids something to be proud of.

5. Take them to a playground if the parents say it's OK. Simple games like tag and hide and

seek get kids active and help them stay fit (a big topic these days). Dancing with them is great exercise, too.

6. Check in often. Kids aren't as good at regulating their time as adults are, and often forget to perform basic bodily necessities. Check once every hour or so to see if they need to go to the bathroom, need water to drink, are tired, or are hungry. Most of the time they won't think to tell you these things on their own, so always be sure to ask.

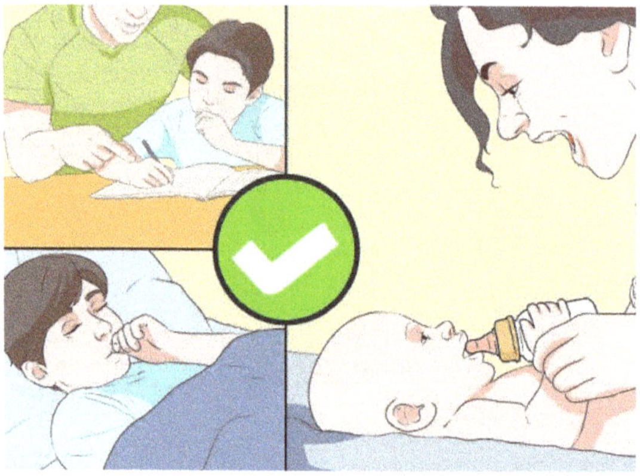

7. Follow the schedule. Assuming the parents gave you a basic outline of daily activities, you should be sure you are keeping up with it. Make sure you are feeding the kid(s) at proper meal times, giving them naps, having them do their homework on schedule, etc.

8. Watch a movie. If there is time watch a movie with the kids. I suggest you watch a movie towards the end to settle the children down before their parents arrive.

- Tarzan
- Finding Nemo
- Avengers
- Barbie Dolls
- Cinderella

9. Take the children out back. Play tag or something to get the children's energy out before their parents get home. Make sure to Calm the children down afterwards.

- Tag
- Duck, Duck Goose
- Hide And Seek

10. Make up a handshake. Make up a simple handshake with the children.

## Part 4

### Avoiding Mistakes

1. Never leave the kid(s) alone. No matter what the circumstances are, your job as a babysitter is to watch the kids in their home - so you shouldn't need to leave them. Make sure you never leave the kids alone in the house. Being in a different room is fine, but running up to the store for ingredients or taking a walk without them is out of the question. This applies even for older children, unless the parents gave you explicit directions stating that they could be home alone for a small period of time.

2. Don't bring people over to the house. Unless the kids have friends who were pre-planned on coming over, no one should enter the home at any point during your stay. You should not have people - friends or family - coming over to spend time hanging out while you should be working. It can be tempting to invite a friend over late at night while the kids are asleep, but even this is off limits.

3. Don't abuse electronics use. With cell-phones, tablets, and laptops more prevalent now than ever, it can be easy to get caught up texting friends or scrolling through social media. Just like many jobs - your electronics should be turned off or used only in case of emergency. You are being paid to watch the kids, not to talk to friends.

4. Don't play movies/TV on repeat. Kids will often ask to just watch movies or TV, and while these may be appropriate in short allotments, several hours of them becomes laziness. If the parents haven't set an electronics maximum, try to keep it at two hours or less. The kids will enjoy having someone to play with, and the parents won't think that you're lazy or slacking on the job.

5. Never answer the door unless you are expecting someone and only when you make sure that it is that person. Peek out of the peephole or window (do not open the door) first before answering

the door. The person at the door may be a stranger. Ask the parents if they are expecting anyone before they leave.

6. Clean up before the parents get home. Although it is sometimes forgotten, a major part of babysitting is cleaning up after the kids. You may not have much of a mess to deal with, but if you cooked or did a project, be sure to put everything back in its place. The parents will appreciate coming home to a clean house and will be more likely to re-hire you again in the future.

- Always clean up after yourself. If You and the children make a mess pick it up after you make it. Don't wait until the end to pick everything up. What if the Parents come home unexpectedly. You would want some of it to be clean.
- Play cleaning games with the kid. Say whoever picks up the most wins or makeup a silly game that includes cleaning.
- Usually there is a mess when you get there, pick it up. Everyone appreciates it when they come home to a house cleaner then they had it.

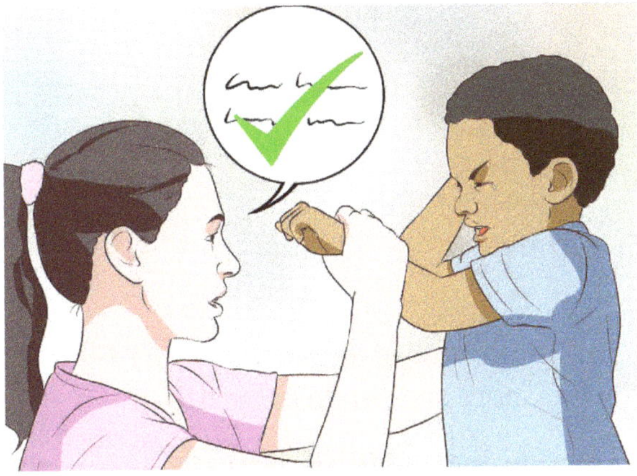

7. Don't let the kids "get away" with things. It's tempting to be the "cool" babysitter who lets kids get away with things parents never allow. Remember, you're not their parents, so you don't really have much say in how the house rules go. You can't be a child's friend all the time.

- Know when to say no and when it's OK to let something small go like letting kids stay up 15 minutes past bedtime on occasion.

- Kids will challenge you. Pushing boundaries to see how much they can get away with is a normal way kids (even toddlers) learn and figure out where they stand. But even though kids try to fight rules, they actually need and thrive best on structure and limits. So check in with parents to find out what the rules are, then follow them, even if you don't agree with them! Not only will this help keep things consistent for the kids, you'll gain their respect and trust.
- The best babysitters think of the job as a responsibility first, with having fun, or earning money) second. Few things are as rewarding as knowing you've earned a child's trust and affection.

8. Always feel free to call the parents if you feel you need to. It is better to be safe than sorry, and most likely the parents will appreciate your concern.

9. Make sure that you know procedures for emergencies; who to call, what to do, where to go, that sort of thing. It will make you feel more safe while babysitting.

- Get all relevant information regarding emergencies before the parents/guardians leave. This could be emergency numbers, where the main "Home" phone is kept, where a spare door key is. Try not to come off as nosy, and the adult(s) will realize that you are just attempting to help. In this way you can be sure of what to do in an emergency and get the children out. In the event of an emergency, such as a fire, drop everything and get the child or children and yourself out of the house. Do not reenter the house, do not let go of the children and call your country`s emergency number as soon as possible.

# Part 5

## Basic Babysitting Duties

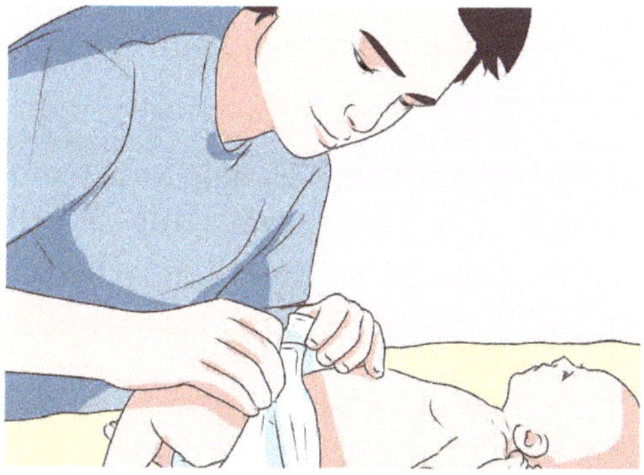

1. Know how to change a diaper.

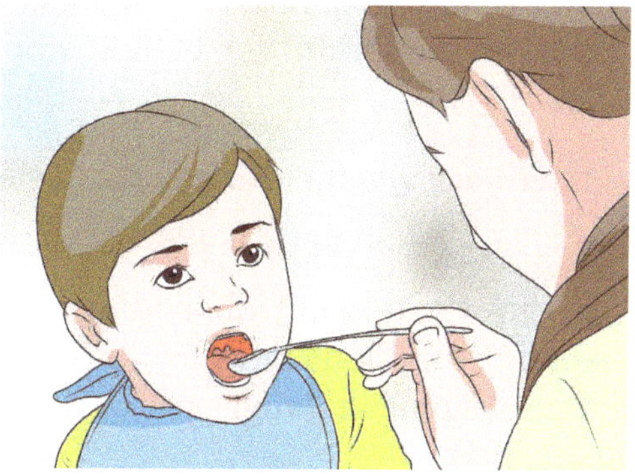

2. Know how to feed children. You should know how to bottle-feed, spoon feed, and keep children safe in the kitchen.

- Feed the children healthy food. It is not good babysitting to just allow the children to eat whatever. Tell them before they get crackers they have to eat a piece of fruit. These things include Apples, carrots, grapes, and oranges.
- Be sure the child doesn't have something they are not allowed to have (such as a cookie or ice cream) too often.

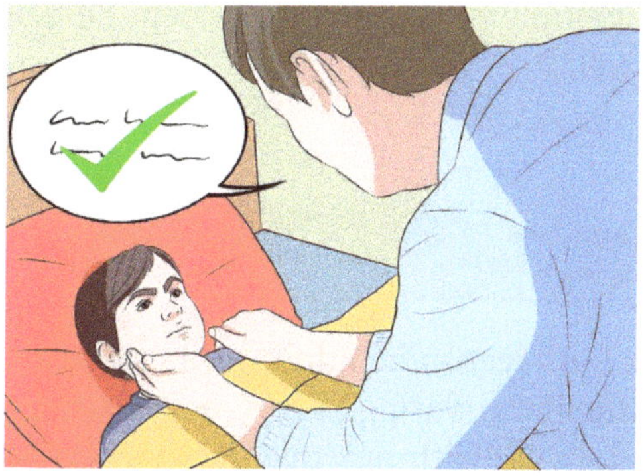

3. Know what to do at bedtime. Be prepared for a lot of whining and problems. For older kids, you

need to know the difference between real problems and stall tactics. For babies, you have to be sure the sleep environment is safe. Here are tips for making bedtime easier.

- Give warning before sending kids to bed. You may want to let them stay up 10-15 minutes past what their parents allow- just be sure they know it's a special treat. Other than that, be firm with when it's time to go to sleep.
- Know bedtime routines. End-of-day routines help kids wind down and signal their bodies that it's time for sleep. Ask parents what they usually do before bedtime. Maybe they have rules like no TV or computer time for an hour before bedtime. If they typically read, talk quietly, or listen to music before bed, follow the same routine.
- Go through the basics. Take a child to the bathroom (or put on a nighttime diaper). Help the child brush their teeth. Find out from parents what else is necessary before the kid hops under the covers.
- Always put babies (and children) to bed in their designated sleep space (be it a bed, crib, bassinet, etc.) This is especially important for babies, who can be injured if their sleep space isn't how it should be.
- Be sure to lay babies on their back when putting them to sleep. It helps reduce the risk of suffocation.
- Before you put the child in the crib, take out all padding along the sides of the crib. Infants should not sleep with anyone else, so don't lie down with a baby who is falling asleep. Don't let babies spend a lot of time sleeping in swing seats or car seats.
- Give the child any comfort items, such as pacifiers, stuffed animals, or blankets, that they usually sleep with. Do not give stuffed animals and similar to babies.
- If a child calls you/wakes up, wait a minute before going in. They may fall back asleep on their own.
- If a baby can't go back to sleep, stroke them gently on the arms or belly. If the baby uses a pacifier, that can also help. Find out what calming tactics the parents use.
- Avoid turning on bright lights, talking, playing, etc. once a child is in bed.
- Remind the child that it's time to be quiet and sleep. Be firm about that final "goodnight" and tell a child, "Sleep well."

## How to Babysit Multiple Children

Babysitting is a popular job for both teens and adults as it can be a great way to make a little extra money. While it may seem a little intimidating at first, especially to someone who has never done it before, it's simple to get the hang of with practice. Every child is different, and whether you're watching a multitude of them or just one, it can be a rewarding experience.

# Part 1

## Planning Ahead

1. Learn the basics about the children. At a minimum, learn their ages and genders. A 12-year-old girl, 7-year-old boy, and 3-year-old girl, for example, will all have different interests, different dietary needs, different things they are allowed to do at home, and different bedtimes. Knowing these things will help you plan out activities appropriate for everyone.

- You could ask the parents something like, "So you have 2 little boys that are 4 and 10. Do they have the same bedtime or is it okay for the older boy to stay up a little later?" Or "do they share similar interests? What do they like to do most of the time?"
- During your first conversation with parents, don't fret about how to ask questions to get the information you need. Parents will most likely be expecting you to ask these questions and may even offer the information without prompting.
- If you feel awkward asking in the moment, simply review the information the parents gave you and then ask your questions afterward.

2. Meet the children. Children are much more likely to be comfortable and behave properly if they are already familiar with you. If you can, try to visit with them for an hour or two a day or so before babysitting. This will also help you get a feel for their individual personalities and how they respond to you and each other.

- If you can't meet with them a few days beforehand, see if it's possible for you to come over an hour or so before you are set to babysit. This way the kids can spend some time with you with the buffer of their parents to make them feel safer.

3. Discuss what the parents expect of you. Many parents will go over bedtimes, dietary habits, allergies, medicines, and dos and don'ts for their children when you arrive. For example, many children have a set bedtime and a routine beforehand, or certain idiosyncrasies like having to have a particular bowl for dinner. Knowing these things will not only help the child feel more comfortable but also help you feel more concrete in directing them if they try to question you or start complaining.

- Be sure to ask questions if you still feel unsure when discussing these things with a parent.
- You can also make a list to go back over later in case you forget anything.
- Remember, if you feel a parent is asking for more than you're comfortable with, you can always turn down the job.

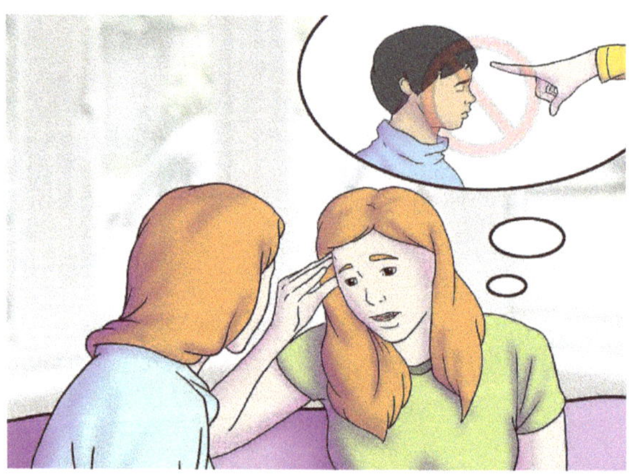

4. Discuss discipline. Though you are likely to have your own ideas and way of managing behavioral problems, it's always best to first ask a parent what to do if their child is acting up. Chances are they will tell you before you even get to this question. However, keep in mind that children act in different ways for different people, and any problems they have when their parents are around may be different than what they do with you. So make sure you are clear on rules and expectations for disciplining their children.

- Asking about discipline can feel awkward, almost like you're assuming the children will do something wrong but don't worry! A simple "just in case, is there any particular way you'd like me to handle behavioral issues? Anything, in particular, I should expect?" avoids assumptions and gives the parents a chance to explain their approaches to discipline.

5. Get emergency information. You should get the emergency contact information from the parents. For example, if you can't reach the parents on their cell phones, can you call the place they are going or someone else to help you? The parents should have a list of numbers for you before they leave.

- Before you start babysitting it's also good to know the first aid basics like how to do CPR or the heimlich maneuver - just make sure you are familiar with the procedures appropriate for the age group you're watching.

## Part 2

## Doing Group Activities

1. Go outside. This is especially good for younger children who may need to work off excess energy. Whether going to a park or just to the backyard, there are plenty of outdoor activities that you can do together. Try visiting a playground, taking a walk, or even kicking a soccer ball around. Just make sure you check with the parents before taking the children to a park or anywhere else.

- Be sure you pay very close attention to the kids when you are outside! It can be easy for them to wander off, especially in a park with lots of other children. Try to make sure you keep them in sight at all times and do a regular headcount.

2. Play a physical game. These can be done outside or inside and are another great way to burn off energy. Try something like Red Light/Green Light, Simon Says, Tag, or Hide and Seek to get everyone involved. Letting kids take the lead in Simon Says or Red Light/Green Light is also a great way to keep them interested.

3. Build a fort. Let the kids plan it out with some direction. You can also have them direct you as you get materials together and start building. This is a great way to engage everyone and let the kids be creative. You won't need to purchase any excess materials, all you need is pillows and blankets. Of course, you are free to use any other building material like cardboard boxes, towels, couches, and tables. Just make sure you know what you are allowed to use and that you clean everything up afterward.

4. Create an obstacle course. Like building a fort, creating an obstacle course is a great way to

get everyone working together. Young kids also often like competition, so having them compete against each other or against you will help them engage and be interested in the activity. All you need for this is the same material you need for a fort - pillows, couches, and blankets. Just make sure you have the extra space and anything the kids can hurt themselves with is moved away.

- Try putting down some tape for a "balance beam," or to mark off spots where they have to jump from one area to another. You can also have them crawl under tables or through boxes, throw crumpled paper into laundry baskets, or even try walking backward. Get creative!
- For even more space, try doing this outside.

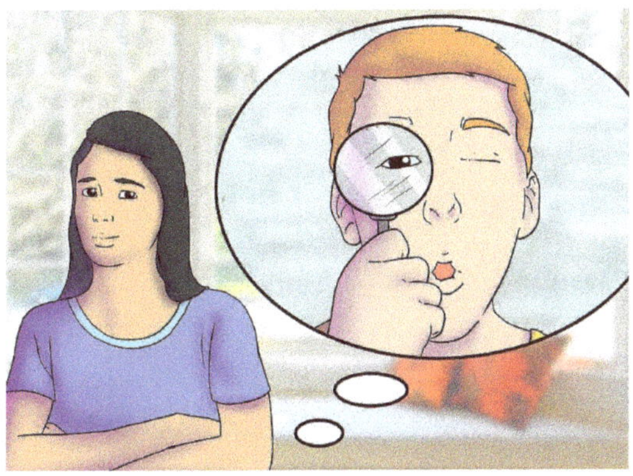

5. Make a scavenger hunt. This can be easy or difficult depending on how old the kids are and how much time you want to put in. You can use anything in the household or bring your own material for the kids. Ideally, you want it to be easy enough for them to understand, yet challenging enough to keep them interested. For younger kids, you can use pictures instead of written clues, and for older kids, you can try simple riddles.

- Write things like "find one gray and white sock," or "bring me two red pens."
- For riddles, try something like "I'm tall when I'm young and short when I'm old," for a candle/pencil.
- Make sure to include some prizes at the end for motivation. These can be anything from stickers to candy.

6. Try painting, drawing, or coloring. If you don't want the kids running all over the place and

potentially screaming, try a calmer activity like arts and crafts. Most kids love to draw and color, so bringing an assortment of pens, colored pencils, crayons, and stock paper can go a long way. You can also bring a couple of coloring books.

- If you know the kids' interests, you can bring coloring books of things they like. For example, a coloring book on Disney's Frozen or one of cars.
- You can also search online for coloring material. The Disney website, for example, has a number of crafts and coloring projects based on their movies. Most of these are free for printing, however, some websites will require you to pay or join to get the material.

7. Have a dance party. Most children love sing-alongs, and if you get up and dance they are likely to move right along with you. You can even let them help you decide on a playlist, that way you are sure to have the music they like.

- If you have enough people, you can even turn the dance party into a game of musical chairs.

8. Play board games, cards, or build a puzzle. These are great for varying age groups. If you have a mix of ages, the older kids can help the younger ones play or you can split into teams. This is also a great way to keep everyone at one table or area so you can watch them.

- Easy board games like Hungry, Hungry Hippos, Sorry, Uno, or Connect Four are great for all ages. Games like Clue, Pictionary, Monopoly, or Battleship work well for older children.

# Part 3

## Doing Individual Activities

1. Try coloring or drawing. This works as both a group and individual activity. A few markers or crayons and some sheets of paper are all you need. You can also purchase coloring books cheaply from somewhere like Toys R' Us or Target. This is a good way to keep one of the children still so you can monitor them while you do something else with the other child.

2. Bring puzzle books. There are a variety of puzzle books for kids of all ages. You can have simple mazes for children or something harder like Sudoku for older children. If neither of these works, there are also dot-to-dot books, trivia books, and even origami books. These are great for children to work on alone or with each other.

3. Let the child pick out a book. Even if they can't read yet, some children are happy to sit looking

at a picture book. For older kids, letting them read a book, magazine, or comic book is a good way to make sure they're happy while you are doing something else. Also, depending on the variation in ages, you can have the older children read to the younger ones.

4. Try building games like LEGO. Not only can children build whatever they want with these, but there are also specific instructions to make things like buildings, cars, or flying crafts. If you don't want to use LEGO, you can also try building with K'nex or Lincoln Logs.

- If there aren't any of these materials in the home, try looking somewhere like eBay or a secondhand store to get them cheaper.
- If you can't purchase these materials yourself and are regularly watching a child or children who you think would enjoy them, try discussing buying these with the parents. They may be willing to pay for them.

## Part 4

### Managing Problems

1. Treat the children equally. If you've brought a toy or a snack for one of the children, you should have the same (or a more appropriate equivalent) for all of them. If you don't, you may run into discipline problems.

- If a child insists that one of the other children got more or something better, have that child divide the items and then let the other child have first pick. This will usually appease both children and make sure it's still fair all around.

2. Separate the children if they can't get along. You don't want conflicts to escalate. Having activities for each of the children to do will make it easier to keep them occupied in this case. If discipline is necessary, review the parents' instructions or use your best judgment.

- Try placing the children at opposite ends of the room or in different rooms where you can monitor both. You can either give them a quiet activity like drawing to do alone or simply have them sit quietly for 5-10 minutes. You can even have them write an apology for what they did wrong.
- You should always make sure to explain to a child calmly what they did wrong and why they are being punished.

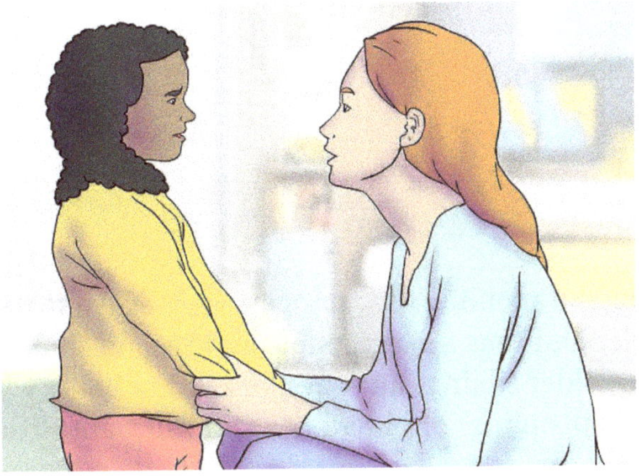

3. Be patient and set a good example. Since children's' needs can vary widely from age to age, you may often find yourself being pulled in different directions at once. Keep your cool. The older children may get frustrated with the younger children due to their differences in cognitive ability, and you have to set the example for the right way to treat them.

- Always calmly answer any questions that arise to the best of your ability - younger kids ask a lot.
- You also shouldn't rush through activities if the younger kids are taking a while. If the older children become frustrated, either have them move onto something else or ask them to help you with the younger kids instead.

4. Place yourself somewhere you can see everything. If each of the children is doing a different activity, try to move yourself somewhere where you can watch them both. If this isn't possible, try to at least move them into the same room. For example, if one child wants to play a video game in the game room and another child wants to color, see if you can have the one child color in the game room.

5. Have the older kids help you monitor the youngers ones. Give them some responsibilities by clarifying that they are older and thus more capable and responsible. It's likely that they're used to doing this as they may be older siblings anyways, or used to being with younger children. Also, most little kids look up to their siblings or older ones and will want to do what they are doing.

- Try to ask them for help rather than simply telling them to help. Simply say, "Hey, could you help him/her with their drawing?" or "Could you please help me run the kids through this activity?"

## How to create a Babysitting Bag

When packing a babysitting bag, make sure that you include important supplies such as a first aid kit, flashlight, and personal items. Secondly, create a template form you use as a checklist to get important information from the parents before they leave. Finally, consider bringing items to entertain and engage with the children in your care. Especially if you babysit regularly, you may want to pack a small suitcase separately that includes toys and activities for a range of ages. Rotate items in and out occasionally, to keep it interesting for the kids. Don't be surprised if they are happy and excited to see you the next time you babysit!

## Part 1

### Including Important Supplies

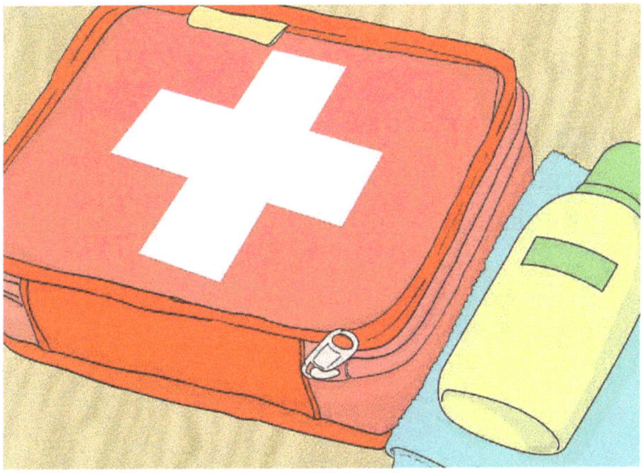

1. Make a first aid kit. You can use a lidded container such as Tupperware or a pencil box to arrange the kit. Include sterile gauze, bandages in multiple sizes, tweezers, safety pins, non-latex disposable gloves, disposable instant cold packs, and various creams and wipes. If you are CPR certified, include a mouthpiece for administering CPR.

- Include elastic bandages with your bandage supply. You may also want to include bandages with color or cartoon characters.
- Pack triple-antibiotic ointment, 1% hydrocortisone cream, and calamine lotion. Include alcohol wipes and antiseptic wipes.

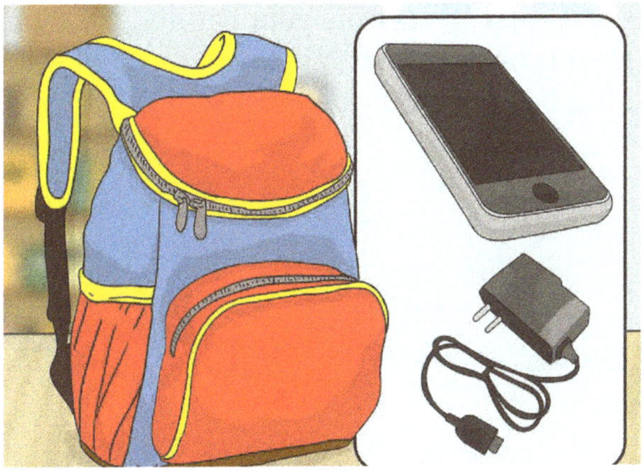

2. Bring personal items you may need. You may want to pack headache medicine in a childproof bottle, and/or any prescription medication you take. Include feminine care products if they may be needed. If you have a cell phone, make sure to pack its wall charger.

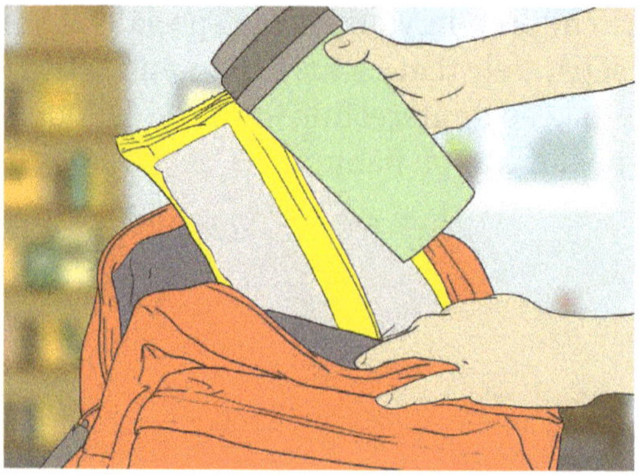

3. Put in your own snacks and drinks. Include a couple of bottled waters. If you don't have access to the family's pantry or you forgot to ask permission, you'll have your own drinks and snacks as a backup plan. Throw in some granola bars or other quick power snacks.

4. Keep a list of your own emergency contacts. In case something should happen to you, you want to have your own emergency contacts on hand in an easy-to-find place. Put your cell phone and the names and phone numbers of your emergency contacts in a quick, easy-to-locate spot like an outer compartment of your bag.

- You may want to remove these items from your bag and put them on a main table once you arrive at the house where you're babysitting. Make it part of your ritual to do this as well as return them to your bag before you leave.

5. Put a flashlight and extra batteries in your bag. This can come in handy in multiple scenarios. If

a power outage occurs, you'll still have a light source on hand. Also you may need to take a pet out to relieve itself after dark.

## Part 2

### Making a Checklist to Bring

1. Collect information on your charges. Write down the parents' names, address, home phone number and cell phone numbers. You should also ask for the nearest cross street or major intersection in case of an emergency. Ask where the parents will be and what time they will return.

2. Get familiar with the home. Find out where the phones are located in the home and make sure you have permission to use them. Ask if you should answer the phone if it rings, and if so, how you should answer. Find out the best way to get out of the house in case of fire. If it's the first time you're babysitting at that house, have the parents take you on a tour of the property. Find out where the children are allowed and not allowed to be.

- For instance, is there a fire escape, or an exterior door that doesn't open which you should know about? Also find out where the fire extinguishers are located.
- Try asking, "How should I lock the windows and doors while you're gone? Is there a security system I should know about?"
- Note where any potentially hazardous areas are, such as ponds or outside machinery.

3. Get important facts about the kids. Write down the kids' full names, ages, and dates of birth. Include their weight, height, eye and hair color. You may need this information if any of the kids get lost.

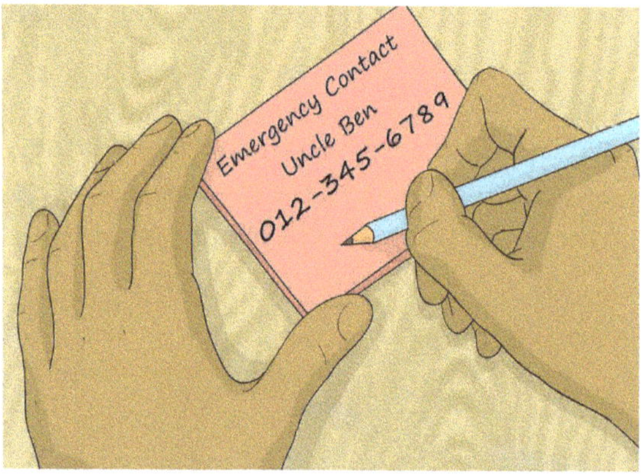


4. Write down emergency contacts. Get the contact information for at least two neighbors or relatives in case there is an emergency and you can't get ahold of the parents. Write down the phone numbers for emergency services and poison control.

- Ask if you should contact 911 and/or a family doctor or pediatrician if there is an emergency.

5. Get information regarding household pets, if applicable. If there are pets in the household, find out if you are supposed to feed them. If so, note the feeding time, as well as the type and amount of

food you should give them. If the pets are dogs, ask if they will need to be let outside and how you should go about doing that.

- For instance, is the yard fenced in? Does the dog need to be on a collar and leash, and if so where are those kept?
- Make sure to write down who the parents would like you to call if there is an emergency involving a family pet. For instance, should you call the pet's veterinarian or a specific emergency vet?

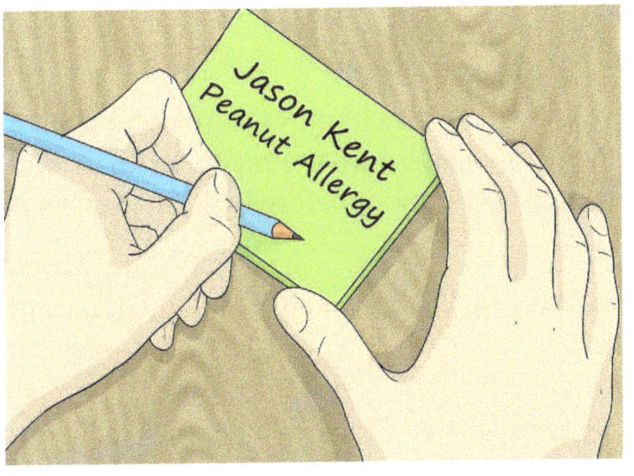


6. Ask about medications and allergies. Find out if the kids have any known food or drug allergies. If so, write them down. Get permission to use over-the-counter ointment or lotion in case of minor cuts or scrapes. If the child has been sick or has a chronic condition such as asthma or diabetes, get the schedule of any medication and dosages they need to take.

- For medications, ask what time it was last given, what time the next dose should be given, and the amount you should give the child.

7. Know the non-negotiables. Ask the parents before they leave what rules you should know about. Ask a couple of questions to get them thinking about what the kids might ask you for that they aren't allowed to have.

- Try asking, "For example, are the kids not allowed to play certain electronic devices? Are there TV shows that are off-limits that they might be asking me about?"

8. Find out bedtimes, if applicable. If your charges are younger than grade school age, they may have specific naptimes. If you'll be staying into the night, write down those bedtimes also. Ask if there are any routines you should know about before bedtime, such as teeth brushing and putting on a nightlight.

- Try asking, "Do the kids normally read or chat in their rooms after bedtime, or should it be all quiet and lights out?"

9. Write down snack and meal times. Ask what the kids should be given for food and drink. Find out if snacks and meals should occur at exact times, and if the children should be eating outside of those times if they say they're hungry. Note any special instructions, such as if their vegetables should be finished before getting any dessert.

10. Ask for special instructions. Do the parents have any advice on what you should do if a child is

crying or colicky? How would they like you to handle any misbehavior? Are there any other special instructions you should know?

## Part 3

### Packing Entertainment Items

1. Pack craft items. You can get simple items at a dollar store, such as crayons, stickers, coloring books and colored paper. If you pack scissors for any crafts, make sure that they are kid-friendly pairs. You may want to get a couple of different crayon sizes.

- For example, toddlers like play dough, playing with water, and drawing with large crayons. Preschoolers enjoy coloring, puzzles, and blowing bubbles. Grade school age children enjoy games, crafts, and many of the things younger kids like as well.

2. Create a "treasure chest." Pack a box or gift bag of small toys. This can be used as rewards for good behavior. Depending on the age of the kids you're babysitting, you can include play money as "reward bucks." The kids can spend it to play with an item from the box.

- Infants won't understand the concept of rewarding good behavior, but you can still include items for them to play with. They like bright-colored toys they can hold and make noise with, and soft items to feel such as plush toys. They also like to be read to from books with colorful images.

3. Pack DVDs. Many kids like movies, so it's good to include a couple of kid-friendly flicks in your bag. Just make sure to get permission from the parents first before putting on the TV or popping a movie in.

4. Consider bringing a couple of puppets. Hand puppets can be great entertainment for kids of all ages. Furthermore, since you will have a flashlight in your bag, you can put on a show with real and shadow puppets.

5. Bring games. Kids' card games are ideal because they don't take up much room in your bag, and they can be fun for many ages. You can also pack puzzles with large pieces. Make and bring a list of game ideas that can be played with little or no props, such as picture charades.

## How to keep Kids Safe while Babysitting

Keeping the kids safe is a babysitter's most important job. If you are going to babysit, whether it be your first time, or you've done it before, read this topic to find out how you can keep the kids you're babysitting for safe, no matter how many there are.

### Steps

1. Keep children under age 5 within eyesight at all times. If they start to go off in another direction, be sure that you follow them, or ask them where they are going, and be prepared to stop them if they are going someplace they aren't supposed to be going to. If a child is over age 5, allow them to stay inside the house, but only in rooms they know aren't off limits to them. If they go outside (make sure the parents allow this), limit them to within eyesight of you only.

- If a child is in another room, be sure that you don't have any TV or stereos up extremely loud, where you won't hear if they need something or if they are crying.

2. Keep them close. If you are at a public place with a lot of people, then be sure that you keep them close to you. Allow them to explore a little if you are at a place such as the park, but always make sure you can see them and know where they are.

- Before the parents leave, ask them if you are allowed to go anywhere in public. If they say no, then be sure that you respect their wishes, even if the children really want to go, as the parents definitely said no for a reason, whatever that reason may be.

3. Avoid leaving a child alone in a hot car should you go somewhere. If you leave the child in the car and someone finds them, and you, then it is possible for you to face criminal charges. Even if you think you'll only be somewhere for a minute, and the child doesn't want to go in, take them with you, as it is for their own safety.

4. Avoid answering the door or the phone unless it is the parents. If it is another person that the parents are expecting, the parents may have a code word or something similar that they use. Ask the parents beforehand what the code may be if they say that they are expecting someone, and if they do not have a code they will use, ask them for a clear way to identify the person.

- If you suspect that there is a dangerous person on the property, then make sure that you and all of the children stay inside and that youcontact emergency services immediately.

5. Supervise children if they are swimming or taking a bath. It is possible for even older children

to drown. Use the bathroom and do other necessary things you may need to do before you allow them in the pool.

- Again, check with the parents before they leave if the children are allowed to swim. If they say no, it is important that you respect their wishes, as once again, the parents said no for a reason.

6. Avoid allowing children, even older ones, to go anywhere by themselves, unless the parents are 100 percent okay with it. If the child sets up something with a friend while you are there that the parents did not know about, although it may not be ideal, you may have to call the parents. They can approve or deny the child hanging out with their friend. If the parents already said no friends before you left, then you yourself can tell the child no.

7. Be aware of all choking hazards. Children under the age of 5 are at the greatest risk for choking, although any child of any age can choke. To prevent this, make sure food is cut up into small pieces, and that you closely monitor the child if they are playing with a toy that is labeled as a choking hazard.

8. Make sure children are not messing with things that could injure themselves or others. Be sure

that the parents have the medicine cabinet clearly off limits, as well as any sharp tools such as knives. If you see the child about to grab something that can be harmful, immediately stop them. If you know that they have swallowed any pills or medicine, then be sure that you contact the poison control center immediately, as they will have information for what you need to do.

9. Know basic first aid before you even start babysitting. This is important, because even if you need to call an ambulance, if you provide basic first aid, that can be the difference between life and death, if the child has a severe injury or illness.

- It is also recommended that you learn CPR before a babysitting job, as this can be important if the child is choking, or stops breathing for another reason, you can potentially save their lives. This, along with basic first aid, can be learned at a class. Usually you can find classes in your area by doing an online search.

10. Make sure children are not fighting with each other. If they are fighting and get too rough, injury can result. Therefore, discourage any wrestling, or play fighting between the children. If they are actually fighting and getting physical, then separate them immediately.

## How to Entertain Kids with Games when Babysitting

Want to be that babysitter that both parents and kids want to hire again? Here's how.

### Steps

1. Ask the parents what they like to do. If you want to entertain kids, then this is a key step.

2. Get all materials needed. For example, if they like jump roping, get a jump rope. Most parents will have a toy or two a child really likes, so ask beforehand.

3. Do the activities with them! You will not only have fun yourself, you'll be watching them. If the children are older, they might want to play by themselves.

4. Dance with them if the kids want to dance! Find appropriate music and start dancing with them. Most kids will love this.

5. Put on a movie. Make sure the rating is okay with the parent.

6. Go outside and play tag, catch or another outdoor game. Don't go out if it is dark or cold. Make sure they are dressed properly; frostbite, hypothermia, and heat stroke are huge dangers in kids. Always make sure children drink a lot of water in hot weather.

7. Ask the parents if you could go to restaurant or order a pizza for dinner. Beware of special dietary needs, such as allergies. Don't let them eat something if they are allergic.

8. Do a puzzle or craft. By this time, it's probably close to bedtime. Don't try to get them hyper.

9. Let them watch TV. Always make sure the shows are okay with parents.

10. About half an hour until bedtime, get them ready for bed. Get them to take a bath, put on their PJs, then have them brush their teeth. This will get them tired and ready for bed.

11. Once it's bedtime, read them a book, put on some soothing music, or sing them a lullaby.

## How to Babysit Kids that are Difficult to Deal with

Babysitting can be a difficult job. No two children are alike, and many behavc differently for the sitter than they do for mom and dad. If you're tasked with babysitting a difficult child, there are several techniques available to help gain control of the situation. By working with the parents to establish consistent ground rules that you stick to, defusing tantrums, and staying calm, you will be fully equipped to handle any difficult child on your babysitting roster.

### Part 1

#### Establishing the Ground Rules

1. Explain the rules and their reasoning. Everyone has different parenting styles and sometimes you'll come across children who are used to an environment with fewer rules than you're comfortable with. To help the difficult child adapt to the rules in your babysitting environment, it's wise to thoroughly explain your rules, age permitting.

- Depending on the age of the child, try sitting them down and saying something like "One rule is that you keep your hands to yourself at all times because I don't want you to hurt anyone, or get hurt by anyone." This works well if the child is old enough to understand cause and effect, typically adequate for children ages 5-10. A 2-year-old for example, may not understand *why* they aren't allowed to do something, but can understand the word "no."

2. Make a rule chart. After you've explained your rules and the reasoning behind them, have the child assist you in making a rule chart that you can refer to when they start to act out. If the child is old enough to read, have them recite the rule they are breaking whenever they misbehave.

- Grab some construction paper and markers and have them help you write out a numbered list of the rules. Bring the chart with you whenever you babysit and put it somewhere visible to the child. When they break one of the rules, stop them and say "Tommy, remember rule number 3? What does it say?" Point to the rule on your chart and have them recite why it is off limits.

3. Explain the consequences of broken rules. After you've explained what is expected from them and why it's expected, tell the child what kind of repercussion will occur if one of your rules is broken.

- You can say something like "If you put your hands on someone else, you will be sent to time out." Or "If you throw a tantrum, you will not be allowed to watch TV."
- Some sample punishments are taking away desserts, taking away a particular privilege (time with electronics), stopping whatever activity they are doing (don't allow them to finish their craft), or taking away TV time or time playing outside.

- If the child is older, say 11-13, more effective punishments might include something like taking away their cell phone, tablet, or favorite video game.

4. Follow through with the consequences. The first time you allow a rule to be broken without the consequence you promised would follow, the child learns they can get away with acting out. Handling difficult children is all about consistency.

- If your rule chart says that talking back to adults will result in not being able to watch TV; you MUST turn off the TV. Even if you were in the middle of a show that you actually liked, the consequence must be followed through, or the difficult child won't take any of your rules seriously.

5. Come bearing gifts. You don't want the child to only associate you with rules and consequences, or they could begin resenting your presence. Try bringing a toy, treat, or new activity with you to each babysitting session. This will create excitement for your time together and can be used as another tool for maintaining the rules.

- Explain to the child that you're not obligated to bring gifts or fun things to do, and if they misbehave, you will stop. For example, bake some cookies to bring with you. Before letting Tommy have one, look him in the eyes and say "I like to bring goodies for you, but I don't have to. These cookies are only for when you're behaving nicely. If you break a rule, you won't get any, and I won't bring anything next time. Do you understand?"

# Part 2

## Communicating with the Parents

1. Report the issues. If you're struggling with a child, the first person you should tell is the parent. It may not be easy for everyone to hear that their child is considered difficult to deal with, but keeping open communication is essential when babysitting. Some kids act completely different for their babysitter than they do for their parents. If the parents don't know you're having trouble, they can't do anything to help fix the issue.

- If Tommy had a tantrum over eating his lunch and threw his plate at you, try telling the parent something like "Tommy had a pretty good day today, but I have to be honest with you, he behaved very poorly at lunch. In response to that behavior, he had to sit in time out for 5 minutes."
- If the child is older; you might be surprised what "version" of the day's events they tell their parents later. To combat feeling like it's your word against theirs, try to tell the parents of any issues as soon as they happen. A quick phone call or text immediately afterwards ensures you won't forget, and the parents are kept up to date with an accurate account of the situation.

2. Get some guidance. Good advice from the parents of the difficult child can be your best asset in combating unruly behavior. Politely explain to the parents that you are experiencing severe difficulty babysitting their kid, and ask them how they handle similar situations at home. Consistency between you and the parents will create a stable environment for the child and help curb negative behaviors.

- Try starting the conversation with something like "I absolutely love babysitting Tommy, but I am having difficulties with a few things I was hoping you could help me with. He seems to throw frequent tantrums, how do you handle these at home?"

- You can also try saying "I think it would really help Tommy if we were on the same page. When he acts out, what consequence do you give him?"
- In the event the parents of the misbehaved kid don't have any tips, ask your friends who have children how they handle tantrums and whatever other behaviors you're trying to deal with. Chances are you're not alone, someone you know has dealt with similar issues and will be able to give you some ideas that worked for them.

3. Create consistency. Now that the parents are aware of the issues and have told you how they handle bad behavior at home try your best to combine their rules and consequences with your ground rules. Your goal is to create as much consistency as possible, even if they have a rule you didn't consider.

- For instance, you may not care if the child runs in the house instead of walking. But if the parents tell you that is a rule implemented at their house, you should add it to your rule chart.
- If the child is older; you may not think anything of letting them watch Cartoon Network, only to find out their parents have forbidden certain programs. Always adapt what is, and isn't allowed while you're babysitting to what the parents do at home.

## Part 3

### Defusing Tantrums

1. Remain calm. You may be very frustrated, but it is crucial that you never take your frustrations out on the child. Remember always to stay calm. When you feel yourself getting upset, stop and take a deep breath. Remind yourself that they are the child, and you are the adult who is in control of the situation.

2. Give them some space. Assuming no safety issues, walk away for a few minutes so that you can continue calming down, while the kid defuses their anger. Once they learn that tantrums don't result in the kind of attention they want, they will stop using that as a tactic.

3. Distract them. Tell them that tantrums don't result in whatever it is they want and try to distract them with something else. Perhaps there is a song you can sing that helps calm them down. Maybe an individual familiar object, like their favorite blanket, helps to sooth them. Whatever distraction you use, don't give in to whatever sparked the tantrum in the first place.

- If you're babysitting the child and their siblings, they might be able to help calm the delicate child down as well.

4. Enforce time out. For younger children, if the tantrum is just getting out of control, time out *is* needed. Designate a spot in the house, whether it be a corner, hallway, or particular chair, to be the "time out spot." The general rule for timeouts is to implement 1 minute per 1 year of age. So, if Tommy is five years old, he sits in time out for 5 minutes.

- If they won't stay on their own, sit with them and make them stay for the entire time.
- Older kids can throw tantrums too, but the time out chair may be far too juvenile for them. For an older unruly child who is getting out of control, it is best to try sending them to their room, or a separate room of the house until they calm down. Tell them they need to sit in that room until they settle down and are ready to come back out and listen. This gives you both a chance to cool off before they return.

## How to get a Babysitting License

Babysitting in an important job. Whether you are a teenager looking to make some extra cash, or an adult looking to do child care as your profession, babysitting certifications can help. Courses through the Red Cross or other online programs can give younger babysitters the knowledge and credentials necessary to both gain clients and take safe, effective care of children. Alternatively, contacting your state's health and child services department can help if you are an adult seeking a state-approved childcare license.

### Method 1

#### Taking Classes at the Red Cross

1. Contact your local Red Cross Center. Most Red Cross centers across the United States offer courses in "Babysitting Basics," "Babysitting Training," and "Advanced Child Care." The Red Cross is a nationally-recognized and widely respected organization, so it is an excellent choice for babysitting training courses.

2. Select the course that is right for you. The "Babysitting Training" course is the most extensive

and effective option. This on-site class last for 7 hours over the course of one day. "Babysitting basics" and "Advanced Child Care" are both online courses. Each lasts for 4 hours, and can be completed at your own pace.

- Babysitting Training is recommended for students aged 11-15.
- Babysitting Basics is intended for students 11 and up.
- Advanced Child Care does not carry an age requirement, but is geared toward experienced babysitters.

3. Pay the appropriate fee. The "Babysitting Training" course, once again, is the most comprehensive overview. The fee for this course is $85. The "Babysitting Basics" online course is $29. The "Advanced Child Care" course costs $49, although it is sometimes on sale at half-price (for $24.50). These fees are due at the time of registration.

4. Attend the class. If you have signed up for the "Babysitting Training" course, make your way to your local Red Cross center on the date of your course. Students are instructed to bring a lunch. If you have registered for one of the online courses, log in and begin working whenever you have a couple of hours to dedicate to learning. When you have completed the course, you will receive a certificate.

- The Babysitting Training course focuses on developing leadership skills, developing a babysitting business, keeping kids safe and helping children behave, and learning about basic child care and basic first aid.

- The Babysitting Basics class focuses on staying safe, what to do in an emergency, selecting age-appropriate activities, and handling a variety of behaviors.
- The Advanced Babysitting course focuses on how to take care of children outside of the home. It teaches students how to keep children safe and happy in a variety of situations.
- You will not need to pass a test. Simply complete the course to earn your certificate.

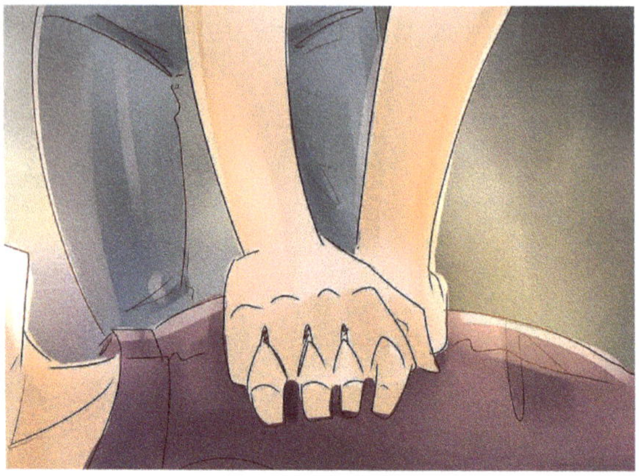

5. Take a CPR and First Aid class. Although it is not required, it is strongly encouraged for all babysitters to take a course in CPR and First Aid. These courses are also offered through the Red Cross. Certifications in CPR and First Aid increase make you a more hireable babysitter.

- The Red Cross Adult and Pediatric First Aid/CPR class meets for 6.5 hours.
- The cost is $110.
- The certification you earn will be good for 2 years.

## Method 2

### Completing an Online Course

1. Find an online babysitting course. Numerous online agencies offer courses in babysitting. Look for an online training course geared toward your needs (such as infant care or early childhood development). Search for an option that fits your budget.

- Free courses generally do not grant "certificates," however, they may still offer valuable knowledge.
- Online babysitting courses range from as low as $20 to as high as $200.

2. Verify that this source is reputable. Although there are many online options for babysitting classes, not all of them may be worthwhile. Look for a company with positive online reviews as well as testimonials from clients. Also, look for a contact telephone number, call them, and ask them some questions over the phone. A company that you cannot reach by phone is probably not a good choice.

3. Make sure you are meet the requirements. Some training programs are geared towards students of a specific age. For example, some are created for young adults (usually ages 11-15), while others are for older students. Additionally, some course like you to already have a background in childcare, while others are for beginners. Finally, some courses require you to be fluent in English, while others do not. Be sure you meet any requirements for the course before you enroll.

- Most babysitting courses are geared toward younger people (often ages 11-17).
- If you are an adult looking to train in babysitting, search for "advanced" courses.

4. Pay the fee. Various courses will have various fees. Some online babysitter classes are as low as $20, and may go as high a $200. Select a course that you feel good about, and pay the appropriate fee at the time of registration.

5. Take the course. Once you have registered and paid the fee, you simply need to log in and complete the course. Various courses will span different timelines. Most courses can run anywhere from 4 to 12 hours. In general, the benefit of these online courses is that they may be completed at your own pace.

- Most courses combine learning modules with short quizzes and tests.
- Once you have passed the course, you will be able to print out a certificate.

## Method 3

### Becoming a "Licensed Childcare Provider" in your State

1. Decide if you want a career in childcare. Becoming a state licensed childcare provider is more

than just "babysitting." It means that you are a small business owner responsible for the health, happiness, and development of small children. Before seeking a childcare license, ask yourself the following questions:

- Do I enjoy working with children?
- Am I knowledgeable about child development or willing to learn?
- Am I ready to be a small business owner?

2. Contact the proper department in your state. In each state, there is a department that handles the licensing of childcare providers. Each state will have different specific requirements for gaining your childcare license (such as age and education requirements), so it is important to contact your state before you take any steps.

- In Illinois, this is either the Department of Health and Human Services (DHS), or the Department of Children and Family Services (DCFS).
- In California, this is the Department of Social Services (CDSS).
- In Missouri, this is the Department of Health and Senior Services.

3. Pass background checks. Once you are sure that you meet the age and education requirements in your state, you will need to pass a criminal background check through your state agency. They will also ensure that you do not appear on the national or state–level sex offender registries (SORS), or within the Child Abuse and Neglect Tracking System (CANTS).

- Each state is different, but you may be disqualified if you have been convicted of a felony.
- You will likewise be disqualified if you have been convicted of a sex crime, are listed in any sex offender registry, or have been convicted of child abuse or neglect.
- Additionally, they will look into your driving record and general criminal history.

4. Pass an inspection. The next step in becoming a licensed childcare provider in your state is for the location to pass an inspection. Whether you plan to open a daycare center or to care for children in your home, an inspector will need to come out and ensure that you meet all the standard health and safety requirements. Once again, these will vary by state, so it is imperative for you to check with your local government agency.

- Contact your local agency to procure a list of safety requirements, and make any adjustments, before requesting an inspection.
- For example, some states require you to have a fence around a swimming pool.

5. Apply for a license through your state. After you have met the age and education requirements, passed the appropriate background checks, and passed the home/facility inspection, you are eligible to apply for a license in your state. Once again, you will need to contact the appropriate department in your given state and follow the particulars of your state's procedures.

# Teaching Social Behavior

# 3

Child care centers provide places for social interaction among children. They can be provided with guidance to uphold good behavior. Providing a safe and nurturing environment is key for a child's cognitive and emotional development. Child care is best understood in confluence with the major topics listed in the following chapter.

## How to Teach Manners to a Toddler

It's never too early to teach little ones good manners. Even kids who cannot yet speak can learn to communicate by signing words with their hands. While learning to share is a life-long lesson for all of us, it's especially crucial during the tender ages between two and four. Likewise, greeting others warmly is a trait that many youngsters can manage when encouraged on a regular basis. Like all aspects in parenting, teaching manners is never easy, but here are a few tried and true tips for sticking with it and being successful.

### Steps

1. Begin with two or three nice words such as "please" "thank you" and "excuse me" and then introduce more as your child begins to grasp their understanding. Children who cannot speak yet are still able to communicate these words by learning a little sign language. For example, when you say "please," make the sign for it at the same time. This reinforces the sign and the verbal word while giving your pre-verbal child a way to communicate back. As you repeat this often, your child will pick up the sign and begin to sign "please" when she asks for something.

2. Be persistent and consistent. This means once you introduce manners, stick with it and rehearse

the trait several times a day. Make it a part of everyone's behavior. It may take time, but young ones are smart and will get it. Teaching manners early in life will pay dividends long after they're out of the house (not that you want to think about that yet!).

3. Model the behavior and language you desire in your child. Children make you better people because they mirror the way you act.

4. Provide plenty of positive feedback when they're signing their words or demonstrating self-control such as waiting in line patiently or helping a friend put away toys. Let them know how polite and thoughtful their actions are to others.

5. Have fun with it. Remember that teaching manners is often the first step in getting young ones to think beyond themselves. Some families have "anti-manners" dinners where all rules are thrown out the door. Try sticker charts to reinforce positive behavior or a "manners" month for those who may need a refresher. It won't happen overnight, but when you see them in action, you'll be so proud. It's not uncommon to first see the fruits of your labor when you're out of the house, around others, or visiting Grandma and Grandpa.

# How to Teach your Toddler to Share

Sharing can be a difficult lesson to teach a toddler. Children at this age do not have the emotional maturity to want to share things because they don't understand or care that sharing will help someone else; however, you can teach your toddler to share — it will just require some practice and plenty of patience. Start out teaching your toddler to share toys at home, then gradually prepare your toddler to share on a playdate. If you start teaching sharing at a young age, your child will be more willing to share as they age and mature.

## Part 1

### Teaching Sharing at Home

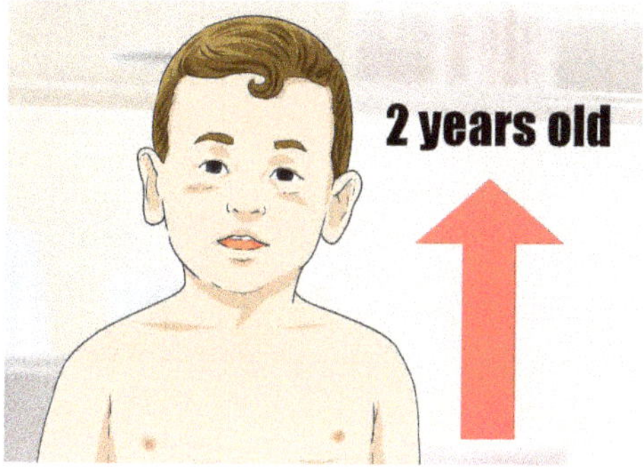


1. Wait until the right age. Sharing requires a certain degree of empathy, which infants and very young toddlers are not capable of. You can teach a toddler in the right age range to share, but it will come through conditioning, not a desire to share. You will have a very difficult time if you try to force your toddler to share at too young an age.

- Most toddlers cannot be taught to share until around two or two-and-a-half years of age.
- Toddlers younger than two years of age will play alongside other children but usually will not play with them. This type of play will not be conducive to teaching how to share.
- Don't force toddlers to share if they're highly resistant. If your toddler gets temperamental, distract them with another toy.

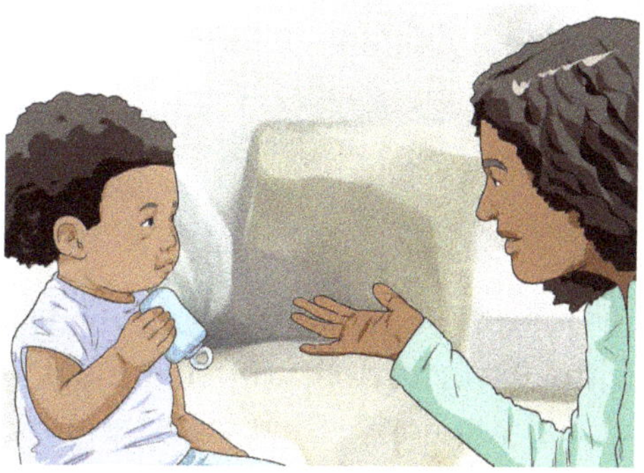

2. Instruct on how to share. Sharing does not come naturally to toddlers. They tend to want things

for themselves, and your efforts at teaching them to share will initially be met with resistance. Be patient and keep showing your toddler how to share.

- You may want to start by having your toddler playfully share something with you. Say, "Can mommy/daddy play with that toy?"
- Ask to play with a toy your toddler isn't currently using so it will be easier for them to give it up.
- Gradually move towards asking your toddler to share with others, such as siblings or other family members.

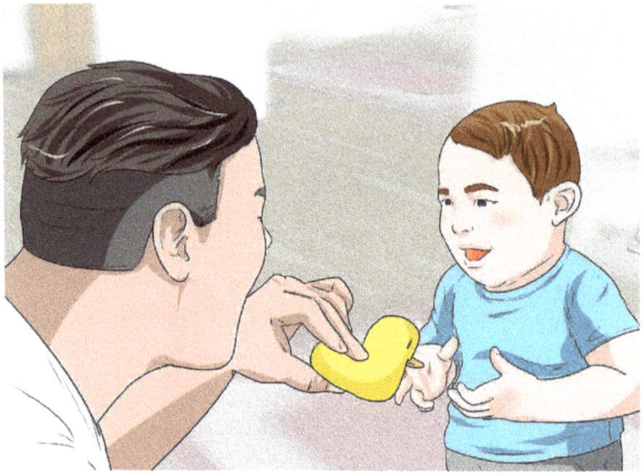

3. Return the toy. One reason toddlers are reluctant to share is that they often mistakenly think losing possession of a toy means they've lost permanent ownership of it. You can help teach your toddler that sharing is safe by returning the toy you "borrowed" back to your toddler.

- Point out that you're returning the toy. Say something like, "See? Mommy/daddy promised you'd get your toy back, and here it is."

4. Have your toddler share with dolls. If your toddler isn't ready to share with other people yet, they might be willing to share with a favorite doll, stuffed animal, or action figure. For example, if your toddler is playing with a car and you notice their favorite stuffed animal isn't being used, take a car that isn't being used and put it by the stuffed animal, saying, "Can teddy bear play with this car until you need it?"

- You can encourage your toddler to directly share with dolls during nap time. Tell your toddler that there is only one blanket and one pillow, so your toddler and their favorite doll (or stuffed animal) must share it and nap together.

5. Make sharing a game. If your toddler is having a hard time learning to share at home, you can try making a game out of it. Set up a situation in which your toddler will be given multiple objects that must then be given away to other members of the family. Be sure your toddler gets one of whatever is being passed around so that they don't feel excluded from the sharing.

- Hand your toddler something that can be distributed, like a bundle of fresh flowers.
- Instruct your toddler to share the objects (in this case flowers) with everyone in the room. Say, "Make sure mommy, daddy, and your big sister all get flowers."
- Praise your toddler for distributing the flowers instead of trying to keep them all.

## Part 2

### Sharing on a Play Date

1. Convey expectations to your toddler. When you set up a playdate for your toddler, it's important to let them know in advance that you'll expect them to share. They may not be expecting it if they're new to sharing, so reinforce your sharing expectations the first few times you institute sharing, and be sure to give your toddler at least a full day (or a few) to prepare.

- If you arrange a playdate or take your toddler to daycare, reinforce that sharing is expected. You can start conveying these expectations a few days in advance to prepare your child.
- If giving multiple days' notice, remind your toddler each day. Say something like, "When your friend comes over, you're going to have to share your toys."

2. Put special toys away. If you try to teach sharing by making your toddler part with their favorite toy, it will not end well. Toddlers may begrudgingly share some toys if you force them to, but they will not willingly give up a special toy that is one of their favorites.

- Ask your toddler for input as you decide which toys are too special to share. This will make your toddler feel like they have a say in the matter.

3. Set out enough toys for both toddlers. Give the toddlers two of each toy. Make sure they're all of the same type of theme so that both toddlers are playing the same types of games and will want the same types of toys. This may not prevent conflicts, but it can certainly reduce the likelihood of them happening.

- Encourage your toddler and their playmate to exchange toys of the same type and share for a while. Do this in small doses, especially if they're reluctant or resistant.
- Only provide two of each toy type if there are two toddlers. If there are three sets of toys among two toddlers, for example, one toddler may want to have two and will only give the other toddler one.

- Be sure the toys are similar to prevent squabbles. For example, you might provide two balls of Playdough and two boxes of dolls or cars (or whatever your toddlers play with), or if they'll be playing in a sandbox, leave two buckets and shovels out.

4. Start with things that are easy to share. Your toddler may have a hard time jumping right into sharing desirable toys, especially if they're new to the concept of sharing. One way to ease your toddler into sharing is to create situations where your toddler won't realize that they're sharing.

- Have your toddler and their playmate share a couch, chair, beanbag, or floor space.
- Encourage sharing by giving both toddlers bubble wands and making them share the bottle or cup full of bubble soap. This is best done outdoors to prevent spills and stains.
- If using bubbles, you can gradually work towards sharing the same wand and bottle. Hold the wand, dip it in the bottle, and have the two toddlers take turns blowing bubbles while you continue to hold everything.
- Point out that your toddler and their playmate are sharing the bubbles, the wands, and the couch or chair.

5. Teach your toddler to wait and take turns. If your toddler is reluctant to share a toy, frame it as an issue of waiting their turn rather than giving something up. Say something like, "I promise you will get your doll back. Right now your friend is playing with it, but you will have a turn after her."

- Try setting a timer for two to five minutes.

- Tell your toddler, "When the timer goes off, you have to give the toy up. But when it goes off after that, you'll get it back."
- Take away any toy your toddler refuses to share. Leave it on a shelf out of reach and tell your toddler, "The toy will stay there until you can share it."

6. Praise good sharing. Real, altruistic sharing will take several years and a lot of practice; however, any time your toddler successfully shares something, even for short periods of time, you should offer praise.

- Tell your toddler, "You did a great job sharing your toy today."
- Consider using gold stars on a chart that leads up to a reward if your toddler successfully shares a certain number of times. For example, you might say that after the tenth gold star sticker, your toddler some extra special play time, such as a movie or a trip to the park.

7. Address bad behavior. Even if things are off to a good start, there's a chance one toddler may refuse to share or snatch a toy away from the other toddler. If this happens, you'll need to step in to defuse the situation.

- If one toddler refuses to share a toy, try distracting them with a different toy. If this doesn't work, you can try distracting the toddler with a game, or try moving the entire playdate to another room to disrupt their social dynamic.
- If the toddlers are snatching a particular toy or fighting over it, you can either take the toy away and hide it, offer a duplicate (or something similar to it) to one of the toddlers, or end the playdate early.

## Part 3

### Continuing your Lessons

1. Lead by example. Your child may be young, but they will still recognize when you're saying one thing and doing another. You obviously share countless things each day, but it's important that you point these things out to your toddler so that they understand what you're doing.

- Every time you lend something to someone else, even for a few minutes' use, explain to your toddler that you're sharing.
- Say something like, "Did you see that? Mommy/daddy is sharing the newspaper because it's nice to share."

2. Talk about your toddler's feelings. Your toddler may be afraid of sharing because they think that they won't get a turn, or that they'll never see that toy again. You can help calm some of these fears by talking to your toddler about their feelings and identifying the roots of them.

- Ask your toddler, "Why don't you want to share? Are you afraid you won't get to play with it?"
- Remind your toddler that they and their playmates can both use the same toy. Then ask your toddler if they can think of any ways to make that easier.

3. Read about sharing. Some books are designed for toddlers ages one to three years old. These books cover a number of subjects, including sharing. These types of books can help reinforce what you teach your toddler by covering a variety of sharing scenarios.

- Get your toddler involved in reading the book by having them turn the pages and ask or answer questions about what's happening on each page.
- Read the book for several days in a row, especially in a lead-up to a playdate with another toddler.
- If your toddler refuses to share while playing with another child, remind your toddler of the lessons from the book. Say something like, "What happened in your book when the bear wouldn't share with anyone?"

4. Be patient. Sharing, even at home with a parent, will take time and work on your part. It will likely take much longer to teach your toddler to share with others outside the family. Your toddler may share begrudgingly if you instill these lessons, but don't expect your child to share out of generosity until at least three to five years of age.

## How to keep Toddlers from Fighting over Toys

Toddlers are just beginning to learn about the concepts of independence and ownership. Sharing, at this point, can be very difficult territory. If you are struggling with toddlers who fight constantly over toys, don't worry – their behavior is normal and developmentally appropriate. The situation will improve as your children grow, but in the meantime, you can take certain steps to preserve your sanity and teach your toddlers how to get along well with others.

## Part 1

### Understanding Toddler Behavior

1. Know that toddlers are working toward independence. One and two year olds are working to master gross motor skills like walking, running, and jumping; they are also picking up fine motor skills like using a spoon, drinking from a cup, and unfastening buttons. These new skills go hand and hand with a developing sense of self: the idea that they are independent beings who can control their own actions. These are normal and exciting developments, but for parents and teachers, the toddler stage is a tricky one. Toddlers will engage in many behaviors that are not appropriate or acceptable (including fighting over toys), and adults have to respect their developmental stage while teaching them to respect reasonable limits.

- According to Erik Erikson, the psychologist who developed a widely-used theory of psychosocial development, toddlers are in the midst of resolving a particular developmental crisis: "Autonomy (Independence) vs. Doubt (or Shame)." In other words, they are working to resolve the tensions between self confidence and self control.

2. Accept that toddlers are highly emotional. Emotions tend to run high during the toddler years. They feel tremendous excitement about all of the new and different things they are able

to do, but, at the same time, they have to deal with "separateness." Parents may leave them to play independently or expect them to occupy themselves temporarily, and this separation can be scary.

3. Understand that normal toddler development leads to fights over toys. The concept of independence, of course, hinges on the basic understanding of "me." Once toddlers understand the distinction between themselves and others, they also begin to focus on the concept of ownership: "mine" as opposed to "not mine." Fighting over toys is a completely normal manifestation of this emerging knowledge. Sharing threatens toddlers' perceived ownership of particular items.

## Part 2

### Teaching the Concept of Sharing

1. Explain sharing to your toddlers. Emphasize that sharing is temporary: another child may take a turn with his or her toy, but eventually, it will be returned.

- Note that sharing does not take away ownership. It's fine to make this explicit for toddlers. Say, "that is your truck. You can let someone else play with your truck, but it is still yours."

2. Practice sharing. Before you expect toddlers to share their toys with other children, they can practice sharing with you. Ask toddlers, from time to time, to hand you their favorite toys. Let them learn to be patient. Return their toys after a designated interval, and praise them for sharing. This will help toddlers distinguish between borrowing and taking.

3. Emphasize the positive aspects of sharing. Point out that sharing a toy is generous and kind. In addition, point out that other children will also share their toys. Everyone will get to play with new and different items.

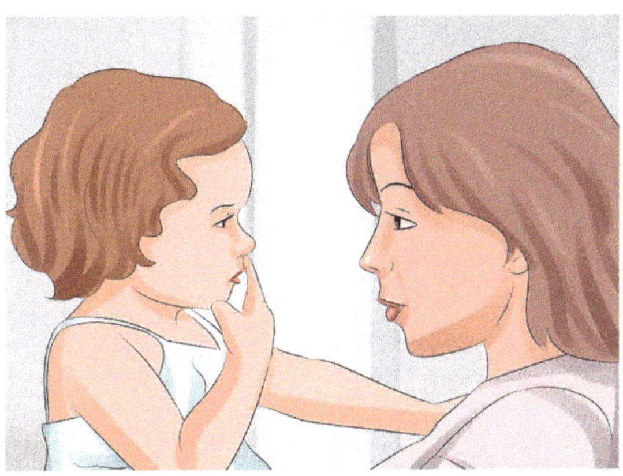

4. Prepare toddlers in advance for situations that will involve sharing. Talk to children about what will be expected during play dates and at preschool. Let them know ahead of time that they will be sharing toys.

5. Teach the importance of friendship. Explain what friendship is, and teach toddlers that friendships involve sharing toys and playing together without fighting.

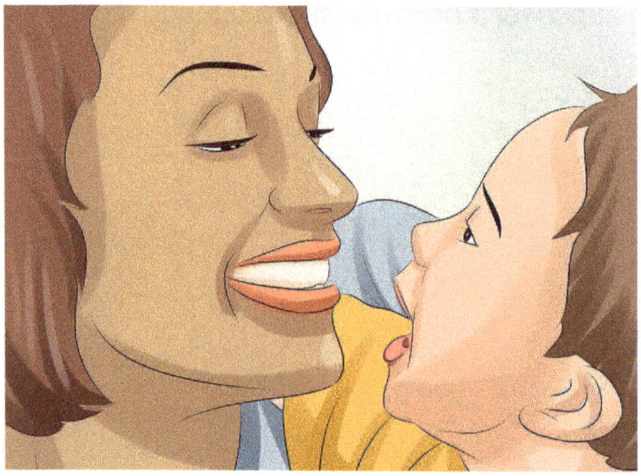

6. Observe your toddlers' behavior. It helps to be aware of what a particular toddler is struggling with. Does the toddler tend to grab toys away from other children, or does he or she struggle with other children taking toys? Teach toddlers to deal with these issues as best they can.

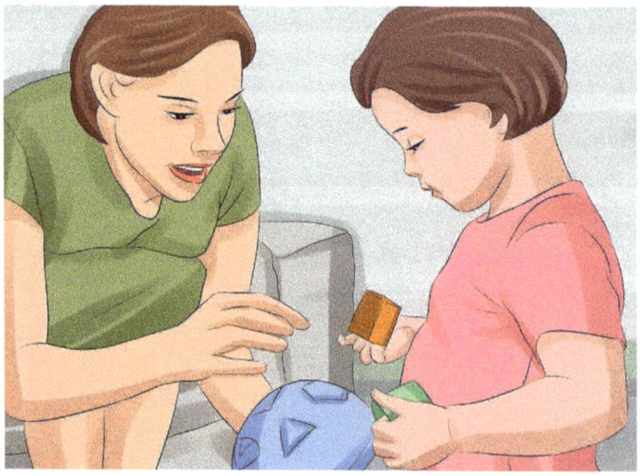

7. Lead by example. Let toddlers see you sharing your possessions with others. If they ask to play with something of yours (assuming that it is safe and not easily damaged), let them. Emphasize the fact that sharing is temporary, and you know you will get the item back soon.

## Part 3

### Avoiding Conflict

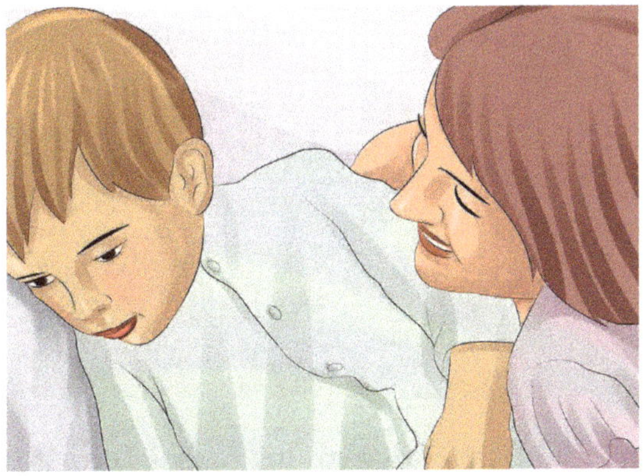

1. Avoid unnecessarily stressful situations. Once you have observed situations involving sharing, you should be able to determine which issues seem to cause trouble for particular toddlers. Is one child especially protective of a particular toy? Consider letting him or her put that toy away somewhere, off limits, during a play date.

2. Choose your play time wisely. Plan to let toddlers play together when they are rested and when they have been fed. Hungry, tired, cranky toddlers are guaranteed to fight over toys. Limit play time to one to two hours for toddlers; anything longer is expecting too much from a young child.

3. Set clear rules. Whenever toddlers are playing together, it is best to have clear, simple rules in place.

Any toys that are not meant to be shared should be put away elsewhere. All remaining toys should then be shared, with no exceptions. Consider setting a timer for popular toys, and enforce consistent limits.

4. Offer alternatives. When a child has to give up his or her favorite toy temporarily, offer interesting replacements. If you give a toddler something fun to do, he or she may be too distracted to argue about the original toy.

- Generally, it's best to have lots of choices available. Have enough options around to have multiple alternatives for each toddler.

5. Teach toddlers to discuss sharing verbally. Instead of grabbing toys from other children, toddlers should be taught to ask for them. Model appropriate language for toddlers: "may I have a turn, please?"

6. Encourage cooperative play. If toddlers play a game that requires more than one person, whether it's a ball game or a board game, they will be less likely to fight.

# Part 4

## Dealing with Fights

1. Try not to get involved immediately. When squabbles break out between toddlers, it's tempting to step in immediately. It's better, however, to give toddlers the chance to learn and grow. Let them try to resolve the conflict themselves.

2. Remember the three "C"s: compassion, conviction, and consequences. If the toddlers cannot resolve the conflict themselves – as will often be the case – try to keep these three basic concepts in mind. Have compassion for what toddlers are experiencing and struggling with. Respect their convictions, but emphasize the fact that their actions have consequences.

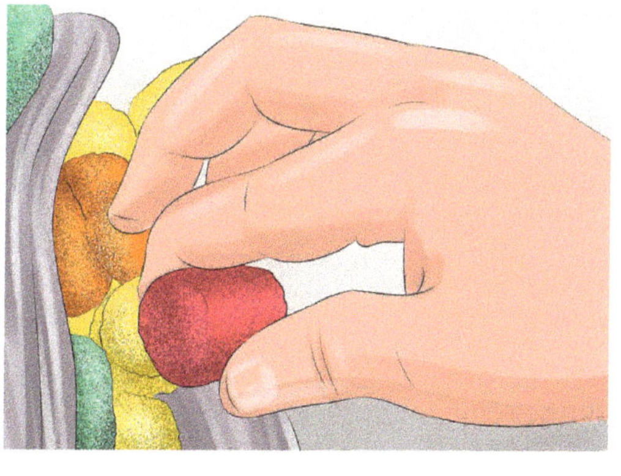

3. Control grabbing. When toddlers continue to fight over toys, it's best to separate them and give them time to cool down. Do not allow them to continue snatching toys back and forth. Wait until

everyone is calm, and then try to piece together what happened – not so much to determine who is "guilty" but to find an acceptable solution to the problem.

- To separate children, simply hold their hands firmly and lead them to separate areas. Ask them to stay put, and insist that they obey. Make sure everyone is calm before you allow them to leave their separate corners.

4. Remove the object of dispute. If you cannot find a suitable solution, or if the toddlers involved are too upset to discuss the issue, remove the toy. Take it from them as gently and politely as possible, and then put it out of their reach. Ignore any shrieking or crying that results.

5. Make decisions with (rather than for) toddlers. When you step in to resolve arguments, you should give reasons for your actions. Allow toddlers to express themselves, and listen to them. Try to involve them in the decision-making process.

6. Validate toddlers' feelings. In general, it's best to approach fights over toys with compassion and

understanding. Let toddlers know that their feelings are valid. It's fine to say, "I know it makes you sad and angry to share this truck, and that's okay. It's fine to be sad and angry. But you need to be a good friend and let Johnny have a turn."

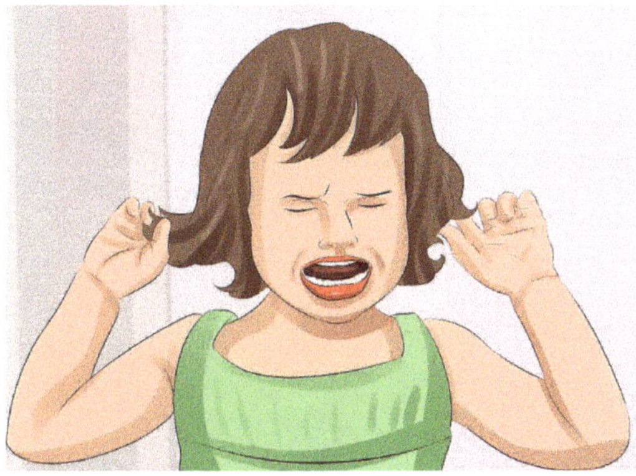

7. Deal with emotions before you try to teach a lesson. If one or more of the toddlers is very upset, you need to take time to calm that child down and validate his or her feelings before you attempt to teach a lesson about sharing. When children are upset, they cannot focus well on learning; they will just get more upset if you try to scold or lecture them.

8. Refrain from taking sides. Remain neutral, and don't pay too much attention to which child started the argument. Even if one toddler is clearly wrong, it's not going to help much to discuss it. Focus on finding a solution.

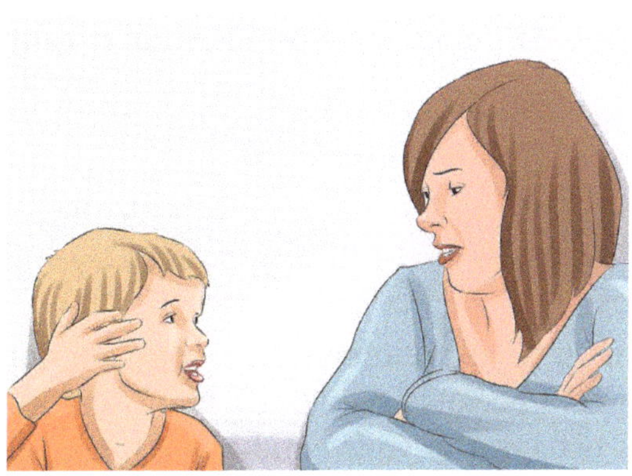

9. Resist the urge to label children. Even if one particular toddler is frequently the cause of fights

over toys, it helps nothing to label him or her as a "bully" or "meanie." You should not call children "selfish" or "greedy," and you should never call them names. Doing so may affect their self esteem and confidence. Furthermore, if you call a child a bully, he or she may start believing it; this will only lead to more of the behavior that you are trying to stop.

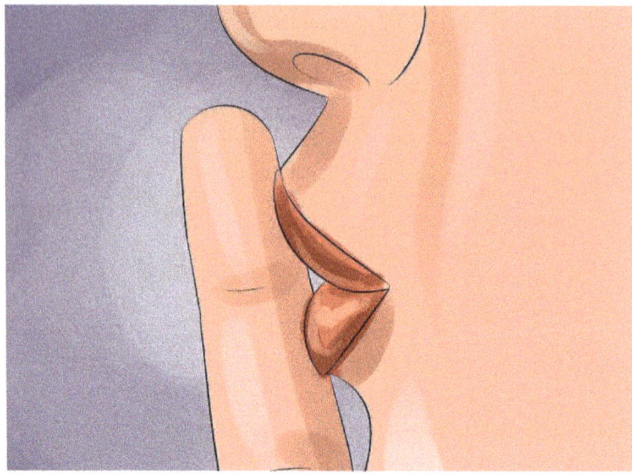

10. Enforce consequences. Depending on the situation, you can try enforcing ten to fifteen minutes of quiet time (placing toddlers in their cribs works well for this) or removing the toy in question.

11. Praise toddlers when they comply. When toddlers are calm and cooperative again, offer lots of praise. Give them hugs and congratulate them for learning to calm themselves down and work together.

## How to stop Aggressive Toddler Behavior

Aggressive behavior is common in all toddlers. They may act out by yelling or hitting when they are upset, frustrated, or sad because they don't know how else to act. When this occurs, you can start correcting this behavior in your child so they can react in healthier ways. Learn how to stop aggressive toddler behavior so you can teach your child socially appropriate responses.

# Method 1

## Responding to Aggressive Behavior

1. Remain calm. If your child is acting out in an aggressive way, stay calm. Don't get angry, yell, or act in an aggressive way to the child. Remaining calm will help your child calm more quickly. If you get upset, that will feed your child's aggression and make things worse.

- Your child relies on you for stability, especially when they are upset. Often, the child is aggressive because they are upset or feel out of control. Staying calm will help communicate to your child everything is okay.
- To stay calm, take a few deep breaths. Inhale and count to 10 before responding. Remind yourself that your child is learning how to control their emotions.

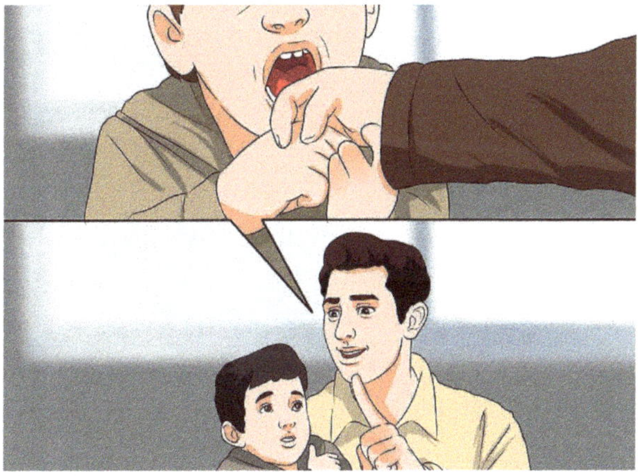

2. Respond quickly and simply. When your child acts out, don't respond in a dramatic or over-the-top way. Don't give your child too much attention when they act aggressively. This may feed into your child's aggression and emotions. Instead, respond quickly and efficiently. Keep your words straight to the point, and try to redirect your child's actions. If that doesn't work, take them away from the situation.

- Trying to talk to your child and giving them a lot of attention if they are aggressive or throwing a tantrum may reinforce negative behavior.

- For example, if your child is biting another child, say in a firm tone, “No, you don’t bite people. Biting hurts.”
- Toddlers will probably hit, bite, or act out multiple times, so remember to repeat your point over and over until they understand.
- To redirect your child, after you have corrected the behavior, try saying, “Why don’t we go down the slide?” or, “Pick up your doll and let’s continue playing.”

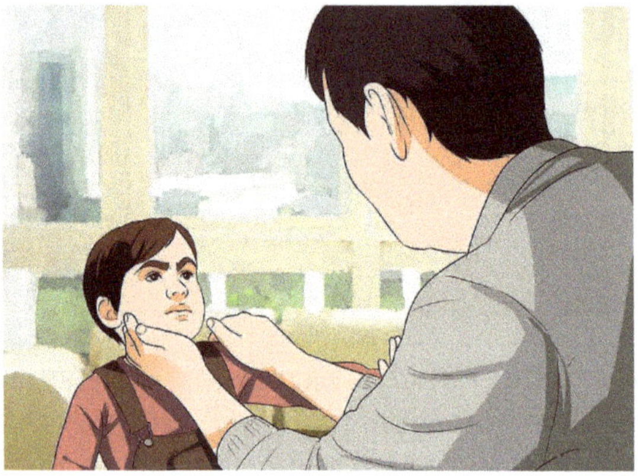

3. Acknowledge your child’s feelings. Your child acts in an aggressive way because they are angry or upset about something. When they act in this manner, acknowledge their feelings; however, you should follow this up with how aggressive behavior is not an appropriate response to their feelings.

   - For example, if your toddler gets angry, you can say, “I understand that you are angry because the other kid took your toy, but hitting someone is not okay;” or, “I know you are upset because we have to leave when you want to play, but you cannot kick and scream.”

4. Back up your words with actions. When you correct your toddler’s aggressive behavior, use an authoritative, strong tone. Sometimes, words may not be enough with a toddler. Use actions along with your words to get your point across.

   - For example, when you tell your toddler to stop hitting or snatching, hold their arm in place to emphasize they aren’t supposed to use their hands.

- Make sure to be firm and authoritative, but not angry or aggressive.
- This may take many repetitions before your child corrects the behavior.

## Method 2

### Managing Aggressive Behavior

1. Set consistent consequences. One way to discourage aggressive behavior is to have clear, consistent consequences for aggressive actions. This helps the child learn that there are negative consequences if they do something. By not giving in to tantrums or negative behavior, you are not rewarding this destructive behavior.

- For example, if your child starts hitting you because you want to leave the park, don't let them stay at the park to avoid a tantrum. Instead, take them home and take away a toy or give them another consequence. This will help them realize that throwing a tantrum and hitting doesn't get them what they want.

2. Teach your child how to let out their feelings. Aggressive behavior usually stems from a child's inability to deal with their strong feelings and their lack of control. You can teach your child how to manage these emotions in a more constructive, healthy, non-aggressive way.

- For example, you can teach your child to punch a stuffed animal or bean bag instead of hitting a person when they are mad. You can tell them to rip paper or jump around. You may also tell them to go to their special place alone.

3. Distract your child. One way to help manage aggressive behavior or a tantrum is to distract your child. When you distract your child, you interrupt their aggression with a completely different train of thought. This can help break the cycle of aggressive emotion.

- For example, you may start talking to your toddler about something they enjoy, suggest that you play a game, or give them a kiss.

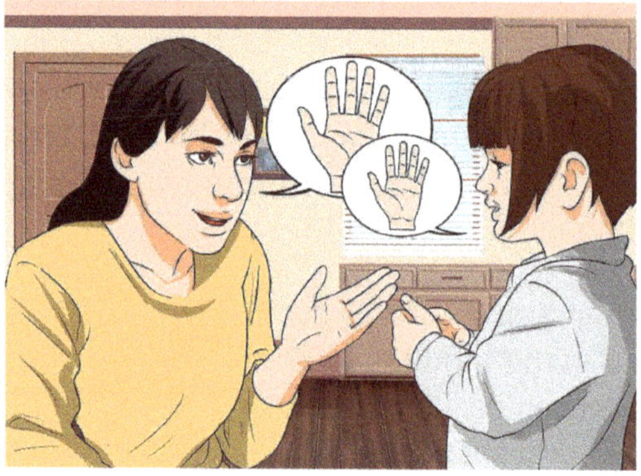

4. Teach your child to use their words. Many times, aggressive behavior in toddlers occurs because they are unable to communicate their frustration or anger. Help your children learn how to use their words. It may be something as simple as the word "no!" instead of hitting.

- Tell your child to say "no!" instead of hitting, biting, or yelling. You can also teach them to say things like, "Stop!"; or, "That hurts!"; or, "That's mine."

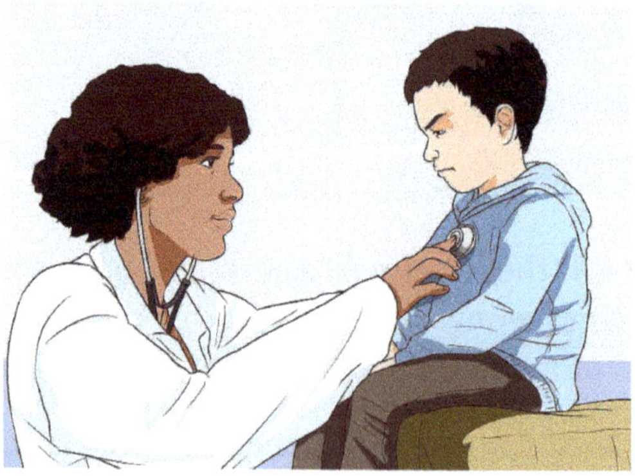

5. Seek medical help. If your child is extremely aggressive, you may need to take them to the

pediatrician or a pediatric psychologist. This may happen if the aggression happens multiple times a day or every day, or if it lasts for multiple weeks. You may also consider it if none of the strategies you've used have helped.

- You may want to seek help if your child is causing physical harm to themselves or others, attacks you, other children, or other adults, or if you fear for others' safety.

## Method 3

### Preventing Aggressive Behavior

1. Try to anticipate the aggressive behavior. If you know what situations cause aggressive behavior in your child, you can be proactive in preventing the behavior. You can try to prepare the child for a new situation or let others around you know not to startle or upset your child until they are used to the situation.

- For example, if you are going to take your child to a group gathering, you may want to play pretend to help them get used to the group situation. Place a bunch of dolls or stuffed animals around and lead your toddler around as you introduce them to your child. Have your child pack a bag and pretend to be going away to grandma's for the weekend to get used to the idea of being away from you.
- You may want to explain to the people at the gathering that they shouldn't try to hug or touch your child until the child is familiar with them.

2. Prepare your child for change. If your child feels aggressive when their daily situations change,

you should let them know the change is coming so it won't be out of the blue. This helps mentally prepare the child for what is coming and reduce the aggressive behavior.

- If you know that you are going to have to go to the store soon and your child will have to stop playing, you should let them know. For example, you can say, "You can play for 10 more minutes, then we have to get ready to leave."

3. Watch out for aggressive playing. You should watch your child as they play for any aggressive behavior. Your child may be playing in an aggressive way, which may eventually become physical aggression. Tell your child not to play that way so that they know aggressive actions are not tolerated.

- For example, if your child has their dolls hitting each other, you may say, "Your dolls don't hit each other. It's not good to hit others."
- You may try suggesting a non-violent alternative. Say, "Dolls love and hug each other."

4. Limit exposure to violence. Letting your toddler witness violence may make them think it's okay to be aggressive. This may be a problem if you have older children who watch certain movies or television shows or play video games. Be careful what toys you let your children play with. Consider limiting the amount of violent toys you let them have.

- Be careful which programs are on the television when your child is around. This includes movies, television shows, and even the news. Some cartoons are violent, so monitor what your child watches.
- This includes violence between other members of the household. Seek help if you are concerned about violence in your home.

# Method 4

## Determining the Cause of the Aggression

1. Figure out where the aggressive behavior occurs. If your toddler is acting aggressively, you should try to figure out where that behavior is happening. Make a mental list of where your child displays aggressive behavior. Does it happen in one setting or many settings?

- If the behavior is only happening in one place, like a store, try to figure out what triggers that behavior. There is something in the environment, like the noise, the amount of people, or even the lighting, that is causing the behavior.

2. Examine when the behavior happens. In addition to figuring out where it happens, think about when your toddler is aggressive. Certain times of the day or stressors may trigger aggressive behavior. Think about specific events that happen prior to the behavior. This may help you figure out what is causing the aggressive behavior.

- The behavior may happen when your child is tired, so right before nap time. It may happen during transition periods.
- Your child may be aggressive right after someone does something they don't like, like you tell them to stop playing or someone takes something from them.
- Being overstimulated is a common trigger for aggressive behavior or tantrums.

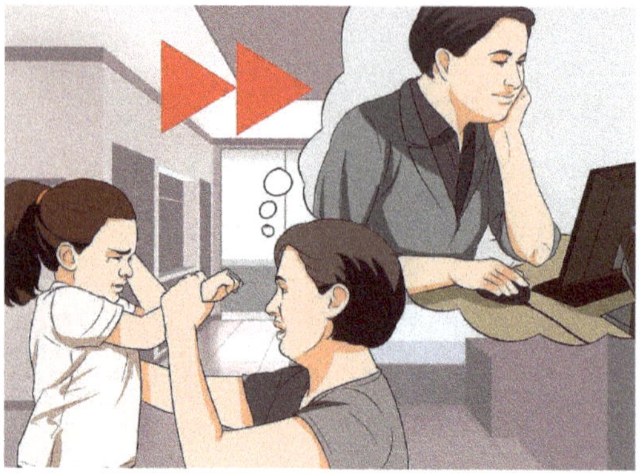

3. Decide if there is another factor. There may be other reasons your child acts in an aggressive way. Maybe your child has experienced a major change that has upset them. The behavior may also be geared towards just one person or a group of people. Singling out the factors that are causing the aggression can help you deal with it.

- For example, your child may be upset because you just started back to work, their grandmother has moved away, or they've switched daycares. The child may be aggressive towards a particular person, like a person at daycare or a family member, or everyone.

## How to help your Toddler Express their Feelings

Emotions can be overwhelming for toddlers, especially when they do not understand what is happening to them. These feelings of helplessness and confusion can often lead to periods of acting out and may even cause regression in skills such as bed-wetting for a toddler who has been potty trained for months or even resorting to baby talk for a child who has a fairly decent vocabulary. There are several things that you can do as a parent to help your toddler not only understand and accept his emotions but to express them as well.

### Part 1

#### Teaching your Child about Emotions

1. Help your child to give their emotions a name. One of the main reasons that toddlers get so upset

is that they do not have a name for what they are feeling. Helping them to give their emotions a name will allow them to express themselves plus expand their growing vocabulary as well.

- Knowing the names for their emotions will help toddlers become ready for the transition to preschool as well. It will be even more important for your toddler to be able to express themselves through words when they are angry or frustrated with the other children they are exposed to.
- Keep the emotional names simple and direct: mad, sad and happy are good starter words for your toddler to master.

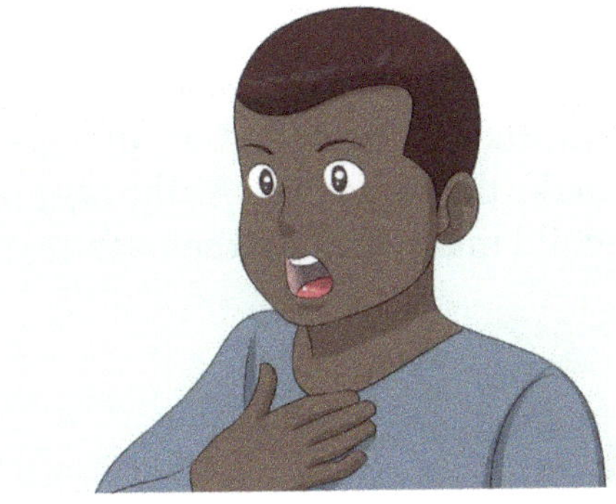

2. Have your toddler express himself with "I" sentences and give him cues. You can ask reflective questions to help the toddler decide the emotion he is feeling at the moment. For example:

- "Are you mad because Billy has the toy you wanted? Do you feel sad that Billy had to go home?"
- Once the child has figured out the correct emotion, you can discuss ways to help him feel better.

3. Use role play to act out various emotions and reactions. Let your toddler come up with a specific scenario and then ask them which emotions would correspond to it.

- For example, the child might suggest a scenario where he does something mean to his little brother or sister, causing the little brother or sister to be sad and mom to get angry.
- This exercise not only helps to work on emotional identification skills but increases creativity and language development skills as well.

4. Play a game where you make a face and ask your toddler what you are feeling. You can also make a face and then have your toddler make the same face. As they get better at the game, you can keep a neutral face and then have your child make the face themselves, then you have to guess.

5. Sing a song about emotions and their actions. The most common song about emotions is "If You're Happy and You Know It", but there are plenty of other songs that deal with different emotions, which you can find on parenting sites online. These songs allow you to go through all of the emotions and possible physical reactions.

6. Read books that help you teach emotions to your toddler. Reading stories is a great way to

discuss the topic of emotions, and many books also have illustrations that will help the child to make a visual connection.

- "Zero to Three", a web based resource site, has a listing of books about emotions and feelings perfect for this age group.

7. Help your child to recognize emotions in others. While you can point out emotions while you are running errands with your toddler, having them point at strangers and announce that "That man is mad!" may be embarrassing.

- An even better and less public idea is to use magazine articles or online pictures showing various emotions.
- Let your toddler tell you what emotion the face is conveying and then ask them questions such as "Why is the baby sad?"

## Part 2

### Dealing with Temper Tantrums

1. Deal with temper tantrums in a calm, controlled manner. The terrible twos is so named because this is the age when tempers and angry outbursts become more common. When a child of this age is upset they may have no idea of how to express themselves and even if they do have the names for their emotions, they may not have the maturity to self-calm and then express themselves.

- If a child is upset already, the littlest thing could send them over the edge into a full blown tantrum. Things like being overly tired, hungry or bored can also cause behavioral upsets and often happen at places like the grocery store.
- It is important to handle the behavior with as much calm as possible without making it worse, but without ignoring it either. The worst thing you can do is give in to the behavior itself.
- Never reward negative behavior just to avoid an embarrassing situation. You will only reinforce that the behavior works and that it should be repeated in the future.

2. Remove the child from the situation if he or she will not calm down. Quietly tell the child that you understand that he is upset but that you will have to remove him from the situation until he calms down.

- If you whisper the child will have to stop screaming long enough to hear you. This may be enough to defuse the situation. If it does not, be prepared to carry through with your words - carry the child out of the store or wherever you are.
- If the child is flailing and carrying him will be dangerous to yourself or others, give him a moment, while monitoring him closely to make sure that he is not going to harm himself or cause any damage in his anger.
- Once he has tired out slightly you should be able to pick him up and remove him from the area without a problem.

3. Have a discussion about what happened. When the child has calmed down, speak to him about

what happened, again, remaining as calm as possible. Use emotion words like "angry" "upset" but do not use the word "tantrum". Do not minimize the child's feelings at all.

- Talk about expectations for the next time you go out and how you can help the child to meet those expectations.

4. Take steps to defuse tantrums before they begin. Being two is kind of a rough deal. Not a baby but not a big kid, children in this age group can find themselves overwhelmed, especially when they are not feeling their best.

- Be prepared with snacks, toys or other items to ward off any potential behavior problems.
- As soon as the child starts being fussy or acting up remind them of their behavior and what your expectations are.
- Give them a task to do to derail the train of thought that could take them to tantrum town.

5. Ask your child what calms them down. For some it is a favorite toy or a blanket. A teddy bear (or other stuffed animal) can be the perfect way to help a toddler learn self-calming techniques.

- Tell your toddler to tell the teddy bear how he is feeling when he is angry or upset.
- When you see your toddler getting emotionally worked up remind him to "talk to the teddy bear".

## How to Build Confidence in Preschoolers and Toddlers with Public Speaking

It's never too early to encourage kids to stand up in front of people and perform. Performance doesn't have to be learning lots of lines for a play or spectacle; it can be as simple as singing a song, telling about a picture they drew, reciting a favorite poem or even doing a Sunday school talk. The more we encourage young kids to speak, the greater the likelihood that their self-confidence will increase with each experience. Everyone has a story to tell and wants someone to listen.

### Building Confidence with Public Speaking

1. Teach the children poems suitable for little kids. Read the poems to them and help them to learn the poems through repetition and even enactment where possible. Then, have the children recite the poems while you're giving them your total attention.

2. Encourage the children to not be afraid and prove it to them by speaking publicly yourself. Even if you are uncomfortable with public speaking, which most people are, your little one needs to know from you that they are not the only one who is nervous when speaking. A child learns by example and does not have the ability to understand the philosophical realm of language and inner struggle. If you only tell them not to be afraid of something, they will agree with you to not do it, but they will not fully get what "it" is.

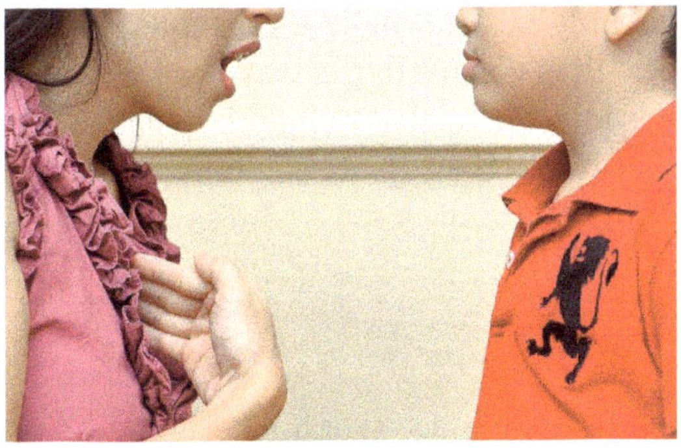

3. Have the kids draw a picture. Suggest that they each take turns standing up and telling everyone else in the group or class about what they drew. Teach them that teamwork and a positive attitude benefits them as well as those around them. This will build self-confidence and self-respect which will make them feel good about speaking in front of people.

4. Teach children to be polite and listen. Have them applaud the speaking child for his or her efforts. This is an important part of growing to appreciate public speaking, especially as not every child will find it a comfortable experience unless they're supported thoroughly. Teach all of the children that it is very important to be kind and to never to laugh or make fun of a speaker.

- Encourage the children to ask questions politely. It is both good for the speaker to learn to field questions from an audience and for the children to learn the skill of asking questions in relation to something they've just learned about.

5. Build a stage for the little performers, if you can. The kids can help with designing, locating and making it. They could help hang the curtain or with making props to make it look like a stage.

- In many cases, it's probably best to make a portable stage that can be put up and taken down with great ease, so that it's not in the way. Use bamboo poles stuck in buckets (stuff paper or other materials into the bucket to hold in place) to create a prop for hanging stage curtains from and a pole across the top of each pole for hanging curtains from.

6. Develop fun ways to teach young children the right things to do when speaking in public. Also demonstrate the wrong things to do. This can be done on a fun basis: Have someone perform all the wrong things like speaking too loudly or too quietly, or too fast, or moving all around the place while talking or facing the wrong way to the audience. You can demonstrate that chewing gum and pulling on their clothes and hair is not the way to talk clearly either. Have some fun with this––the children will laugh a lot but the lessons will still be taken up by their inquiring minds.

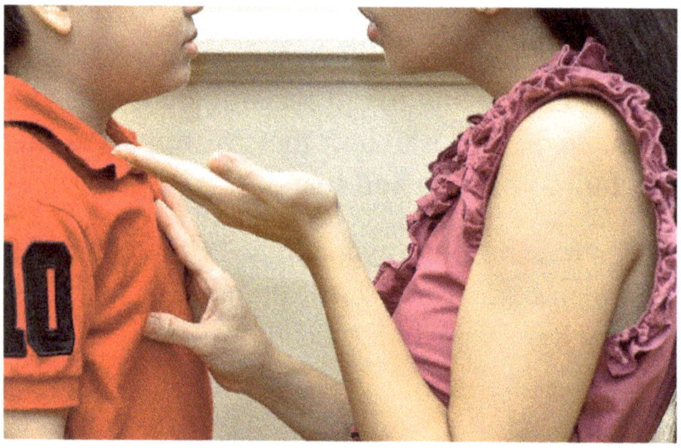

7. Teach the children about "the big finish." That unlike dancing or playing music, public speaking is not about making a lot of movement, or tapping fingers or feet, or fidgeting. Show energy but don't be too excited or boring, but just right, to share their ideas. However you wish to accomplish this just remember to focus on what "to do" , instead of what "not to do" and everyone including yourself will have more fun.

- Some public speakers do walk around as they talk; in fact, some of the most engaging ones do this. Children can be encouraged to be expressive with their hands and walking provided that they don't cover their faces or place any part of their sides or back to the audience. As before, and exaggerated performance these mistakes will lighten the mood and help them to laugh at themselves and not judge others.

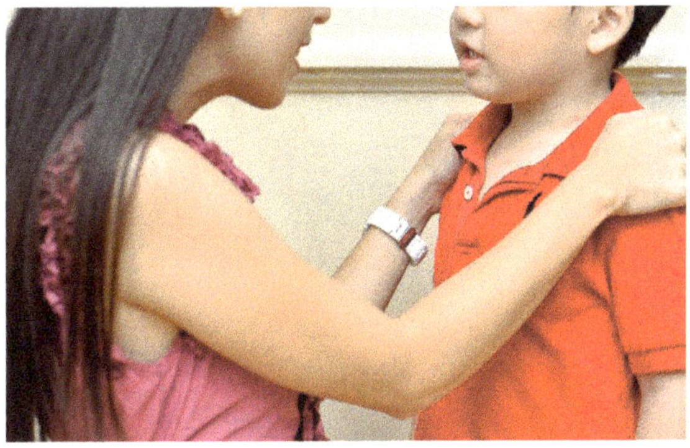

8. Truly listen to what the children have to say. It is important that we teach them that what they have to say is important. If we show them that we value it and want to hear what they have to say they will feel more comfortable and respectful with strangers. Part of successful speaking is also learning to be considerate to others by listening.

## How to Develop your Children's Speech and Language Skills through Play and Positive Daily Interaction

Building a language rich environment is, on the face of it, an easy thing to do. Unfortunately, in today's busy households and with the busy lifestyles of parents who have to work full-time, it is harder to find the time to spend with your children than many of us realize. However, there are many opportunities to use and teach language in everyday situations and create a good environment for learning.

### Steps

1. Make time for your children! Be aware that children learn speech and language through listening, watching, exploring, copying, initiating, responding, playing and interacting with others. For those first few years most of the important interaction is going to be between the child and their parents, carers and maybe siblings. Finding time to spend with your children and have a shared focus is very important if you want to help them to develop their speech, language and social skills. One-to-one time will benefit your child in the long term.

2. Avoid the TV. You are doing your child a disservice if you have spare time, but put them in front of the TV. There are a few (and only a few!!) children's TV programs that are in any way educational. Your child is more likely to learn about things from one-to-one playtime with his parent or carer. TV and video games are passive entertainment and do not encourage any interaction. Studies now show that children who watch too much TV in their early years are more likely to have difficulties with attention and listening when they reach school age.

3. Ditch the pacifier. There is also evidence to show that if the child uses a dummy/pacifier their speech can be delayed. Speech can be delayed because the child is speaking less and the development of the child's oral musculature may be affected by maintaining an immature sucking pattern, appropriate for an infant, but not for a child who is getting ready to eat and speak.

4. Build an environment that helps language flourish. Building a language rich environment is

about using every opportunity to use language, to interact, to share a focus, to talk, to take turns. Building a language rich environment is also about building a nurturing environment, giving your child love and affection and building their self-confidence. And finally, it is about building a learning environment, creating a place where love, language and learning can all take place together. So what do you do to create this environment? Well firstly look at yourself and how you are communicating:

- Remember your language level - One of the biggest things to be aware of when using language around your young child is the level and complexity of the language you use. Think about their age and how much language they use. A young child will generally understand more words than he uses in speech. You can use a milestones chart to have a broad idea of your child's language level. Assuming your child is developing along normal lines think about where to pitch you language. For instance, if your child is aged 2 years and 6 months and is able to follow a short instruction containing 2 key words, be mindful of this when you talk to her. If you use long sentences she will not understand you. If your child does have difficulty understanding, just use key words, more intonation, and gesture, or point as you say the words.

- When talking to your child, try to talk about things that are in context or that the child can see, so they can use these things as a reference. Talk slowly and put emphasis on the key words if they are in a sentence, and use lots of intonation to help emphasize meaning. Give the child more time to respond than you would with older children or an adult. Younger children may need a little longer to process your speech and formulate an answer of their own. This is even more important if your child has difficulties acquiring language. If your child has language difficulties, or receptive language delay, limiting your words, giving them lots of time to process language, and using lots of gesture is essential.

5. Take a step back and feed in language. You can enhance your child's development of language by sometimes taking a step back during play and letting them take the lead. This gives the child control of their environment and builds their confidence. Although you are still involved in the play you are not dictating what is happening. However, you can still be feeding language into the play as it is happening. So the takeaway here is not to feel you have to fill in any gaps of silence, just watch and listen and add language. For instance, if your daughter is playing with her dolls, just watch, add language to her words and dictate some of her actions.

- Chloe: dolly tea
- Mum: the dolly's drinking tea, and that one is having a sandwich
- Chloe: sandwich
- Mum: mmm sandwich, what's it got in it...jam, a jam sandwich mmm
- Chloe: mmmm sandwich
- Mum: mmmmm jam sandwich yummy
- Chloe: more tea
- Mum: more tea for dolly and teddy is drinking tea too
- Chloe: cake
- Mum: oooh, are they getting cake too, yummy
- Chloe: yummy cake
- Mum: yum yum yum eating lots of cake (rubs tummy)
- This is a simple example and although mum is only adding a few new words she is acknowledging her daughter's words and she is expanding on her sentences. Chloe can hear her words being put into longer more grammatical sentences and a couple of verbs are added (eating and drinking). Chloe remains in charge throughout the game, she leads the game and the dictates what is happening. This situation allows her control so there is no pressure on her to communicate and the communication environment is a relaxed and nurturing place.

6. Be conscious of the language you use during play. Children do not learn language by having an adult continually asking them to name various items. Children learn by hearing words and linking them to things. So it is a good idea to feed language into play, rather than asking your child to name every toy they are playing with. Adding language is an easy thing to do and can be done in all types of different situations, not just play. You can comment on what the child sees, commentate on what your child is doing, or expand on what they have said e.g.:

- Child: car
- Adult: that's right, it's a car, a fast car; or

- Adult: that's right, it's a car, a red car,and there is a blue car
- Child: cat
- Adult: yes, the cat is climbing (gesture the actions, and emphasize the key words cat and climbing)

7. Consider that the other way to add language is to describe what your child is doing during play. For instance, if your daughter is playing with her dolls in the dolls house, give a little commentary:

- Jane: dolly
- Dad: dolly's going in the house
- Jane: sit
- Dad: dolly's sitting down
- Jane: drink
- Dad: dolly's got a cup, she is drinking tea drink tea
- Jane: tea
- Dad: yes, dolly is drinking tea... and now she is eating cake

8. Avoid asking a question. The temptation here is to ask a question, such as "what is dolly doing" or "what is dolly drinking". This immediately puts the emphasis on the child, and they then have to stop their play and respond. By just commenting, you are not putting any pressure on your child

to communicate so the play is more relaxed. The child is also able to play on their own terms and control the game.

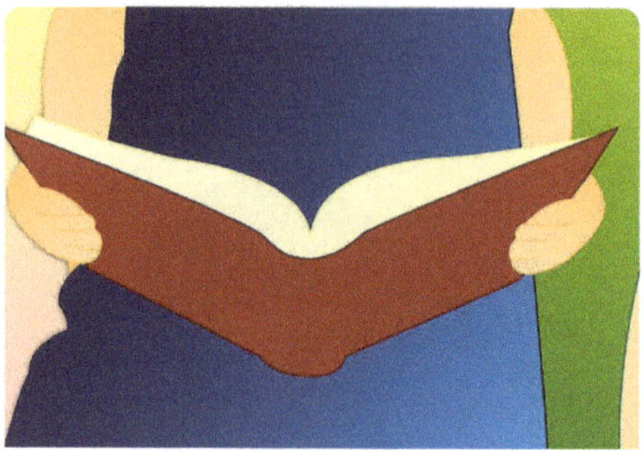

9. Have a shared focus. The above examples show the importance of having a shared focus. This is important because not only are you giving the child a point of reference when you talk about things, but the child is learning listening and using attention skills. These skills are vitally important for the child when they attend school and the early years are key years for developing these skills. The best ways to develop these skills is to spend time with your child, talk and play with child, and have a shared focus.

10. Try to develop a shared focus with your child whenever you are engaging in communication. Share the moment and look at things together. Make sure you are at the child's level and have good eye contact. It is important to notice what interests your child and what they are focusing on, and then comment on it. This helps create a shared focus, shows the child that you are interested and allows them to link language to the things they are looking at when you comment.

11. Make sure you attend to the child's vocalizations or attempts at speech and Try to translate

them. If you are able to acknowledge and understand your child's attempts at speech it encourages them to attempt more, and at the same time you are providing a good model of the speech. If you can't understand your child, repeat back her word, but at the same time point to things you think she may be trying to say. Most daily activities can involve a shared focus:

- Shopping: tell your child what item you are looking for, that way you can turn your attention to the items on the shelves and name some of them. You can name them for your child, if she does not recognise them.
- Reading books: this is an excellent way to have a shared focus. Look at the book, talk about the pictures and read the story.
- Cooking: make a cake together, talk about the ingredients and what you are doing (stirring, mixing, pouring etc). Follow a recipe step by step (sequencing skills).
- Toys: have a tea party with your daughter and her dolls. Describe what everyone is doing (but don't ask questions and let your daughter take the lead). Do the voices for some of the dolls and add language that way.

12. Pretend play. Pretend play is another great way to develop your child's imagination and add lots of language at the same time. Letting your child lead the game also gives them a sense of control and can build self confidence. Here is an example of how a dad and his son pretend to be firemen and all the different ways that this can be educational for the child:

- Example 1. - Firemen - You are a dad and you have 15 minutes to spend with your 4-year old son. You decide to be firemen and imagine that you have got a call to put out a fire in a big building. Firstly let's think about the Language we will be using:
    - Nouns: fire, fireman, hat, boots, hose, water, fire engine, smoke, ladder
    - Verbs: drive, climb, run, jump, smell
    - Adjectives: hot, wet
    - Prepositions: in front, in, on

- Social skills: Turn-taking and shared focus
- Self confidence: Let your son be the chief fireman, let him give you the orders
- Affection: Give him a hug to celebrate when you put the fire out and save all the people
- How easy was that! This is just one short simple little role play where a boy is playing, learning, listening and using language, building social skills, building self confidence, and bonding with his dad. Dad only needed 15 minutes out of his day to do it. It is not hard, you can do it in short bursts when you have little pieces of time.

- Example 2. Dress up for the ball
  - Have a dress-up with your daughter and imagine you are going to a ball. Language used:
  - Nouns: dress, shoes, ball, make-up, hair etc
  - Verbs: dress, dance, fasten etc
  - Adjectives: pretty, elegant etc
  - Prepositions: on, in, under etc
  - Social skills: A shared focus, talking about the ball
  - These are simple examples and with a bit of imagination could be expanded in all sorts of ways, but it illustrates that it is easy to create playtime situations, that are fun and also can be used to positively promote speech and language skills, social skills and build confidence.

13. Observe body language and gesture usage. Try to use body language and gesture when you speak. This helps the child understand what you are saying, but it may also teach them to do the same so that they can make themselves understood more effectively. Body language plays a huge part in helping others gain meaning from what we say, this is a good skill for children to learn, especially if their speech is not clear in the early years.

14. Answer questions. Children are inquisitive and it is important to always take the time to answer their questions. Answering questions creates a 2-way communication process, because you both have a turn and you both have to wait and use good listening skills. Sometimes children go through a phase of asking "why" in response to everything you say. If this becomes a habit (rather than a genuine question), respond with your answer and then ask them a question. This creates a turn-taking opportunity and at the same time making the child to respond to a question. If you want your children to learn language and develop speech and social skills - TURN OFF THE TV AND TALK TO THEM AND PLAY WITH THEM!

# Encouraging Learning in a Day Care

4

Day care centers can provide significant learning activities for the children to perform. Simple lessons can be taught and child participation can be rewarded with gifts and praise. The topics discussed in the chapter are of great importance to broaden the existing knowledge on child day care.

## How to Teach a Toddler Letter Recognition

Alphabet knowledge is how familiar a child is with both the way a letter looks and the sound that letter makes. How well a child knows letters and their associated sounds can predict how well that child will do when it comes to reading and spelling. Children who start kindergarten without a lot of alphabet knowledge may struggle to keep up with their classmates. Therefore, it's an excellent idea to start teaching your child to recognize letters and their sounds when still a toddler.

### Method 1

#### Helping your Toddler Understand Letters

1. Print or buy an alphabet chart. The best way for a toddler to start to recognize the various features of different letters is to practice writing those letters. And easy way to practice writing is to use an alphabet chart on a piece of paper. You can either print them off the internet, or buy a book with these charts. These charts will have all the lower and upper case letters and include arrows to show how each letter is to be written.

- You will likely want to practice writing the alphabet multiple times, so printing off several copies of the alphabet chart will be very helpful.
- It is also important that the alphabets used have properly proportioned letters. For example, toddlers need to understand the size difference between an upper case "A" and a lower case "a."

2. Help toddlers understand how letters are written. Letters are normally written starting at the top, then going down. And starting at the left and then going to the right. It is important that toddlers understand this when practicing their letters. While it may be tempting to use plain paper, using paper that either already has the letters drawn on it, or using paper with the proper lines, will be easier for toddlers to understand at first.

- You may want to start with a pencil as the writing instrument, but don't limit toddlers to only one instrument. While toddlers are learning, use pens, pencils, markers, or even finger paint.
- When teaching toddlers to write letters, stick with only one type of font. Avoid mixing different types of fonts (which may be found on different alphabet charts) so as not to confuse them.

3. Use a description to help toddlers understand the lines on the paper. You will probably remember this type of paper from your own school days, but it consists usually of three horizontal lines, in-between which each letter can be written. The top and bottom lines are solid, while the middle line is dotted. Some letters, like 'g,' 'j,' 'p,' 'q,' and 'y,' will have a part of the letter that goes beneath the bottom, solid line.

- In order to help verbally guide toddlers when writing on this type of paper, it is helpful to name each line and each section so they can follow along.

- One suggestion is to call the top line the "roof," the middle dotted line the "fence," and the bottom line the "sidewalk." The are under the "sidewalk" might be called the "ditch."
- Another suggestion is to use "ceiling," "window," "floor," and "basement."

4. Describe how to write each letter using easy-to-remember descriptions. Ideally, toddlers who are leaning how to write their letters will also remember your verbal descriptions. When they are working on their own, they may even say these verbal descriptions out loud to help guide them. There are no set descriptions to use for all the letters, however, the language used needs to be vivid and concrete.

- For example, when verbally describing how to write the letter 'b,' you might use the following language: "To make a lower-case b, start at the roof, drop straight down to the sidewalk, and then bounce back up to the fence and around." Eventually this could be shortened to "drop down, bounce up, and back."

5. Expose toddlers to nursery rhymes, songs, and poems. Nursery rhymes, songs, and poems are a great learning experience for toddlers as they help teach how letters and words sound. The more you expose your toddler to these items, the more your toddler will recognize rhyming words and sounds without help.

- Around the time a child is three years old, sounds and syllables will become recognizable.

- Also around the ages of three or four years old, children will begin to recognize when two words begin with the same sound.
- This is a great time to teach your toddler the Alphabet Song. And while it may become annoying, try to sing the Alphabet Song every day.
- While teaching your toddler about sounds and rhymes, you can also help teach about syllables by clapping each syllable out that is contained within your toddler's name. For example, if your toddler is named "Alexander," you can teach him to clap four times for each syllable in his name — "Al + ex + an + der."

## Method 2

### Practicing to Recognize Each Letter

1. Teach toddlers to spell their names. Up until now, toddlers have mainly scribbled when drawing or writing on their own. They understand that letters are suppose to mean something that someone can say out loud, but they don't know how to read those letters on their own. In order to help toddlers recognize and understand letters, teach them how to spell their own names.

- Toddlers often recite stories based only on visual clues. The same may happen with their name. It may appear like they're reading their name, but in fact they recognize the visual look of their name and simply know that it means their name.

2. Read to toddlers all the time. Toddlers love story time. And while it's fun for them and you, it's

also a great learning experience. The best way to use reading to teach letter recognition is to read the words while toddlers can see the words in the book. You may even want to follow along with your finger so they know which written words correspond to which sounds.

3. Buy sticky letters that can be used during a bath. There are all sorts of neat bath toys out there, including letters that can be stuck to the tiles beside the bath tub. While you're giving your toddler a bath, play with the letters and help your toddler spell words on the wall. The words don't have to be 'real,' but you can help your toddler say the letters as they're put on the wall.

- This is a great opportunity to have your toddler spell their own name.

4. Draw letters with sidewalk chalk. Using your driveway or sidewalk, write out several letters of the alphabet. You can use any set of letters, but you might want to consider using the letters in your toddler's name. Once drawn, ask your toddler to go to a specific letter (and help direct your toddler if necessary). After awhile your toddler should be able to recognize the letters without help.

- Games like this work best if they're repeated over and over again. In the case of this game, each time should include slightly different letters put in different places.

5. Prepare alphabet soup or cereal to eat. It might seem silly, but the letters of the alphabet that are in cereal or soup can also help your toddler with letter recognition. While your toddler is eating, point out specific letters and ask what it is. Correct your toddler if the letter isn't know.

6. Make bean bags with letters on them. Another great way to help teach your toddler letter recognition is to use bean bags. Each bean bag should have a different letter of the alphabet on it. You can turn the bean bags into a game by asking your toddler to toss the bean bag with a specific letter on it.

- These bean bags are also useful for simply displaying the letters when playing at the table or on the carpet.

7. Use magnetic letters. You can either buy your own set of magnetic letters, or you can make your own. Either way, they can be used on any flat metal surface, including: the fridge, a metal baking tray, or sometimes even a chalk board. Ask your toddler to find specific letters in the bunch, or isolate a specific letter and ask your toddler what it is.

8. Write letters using a toddler's body. A creative alternative to writing letters out on paper, or seeing them on a specific material, is to actually form each letter with or on a toddler's body. Toddlers could lie on the floor and write different letters using their body and other props.

## Method 3

### Using Words to help with Letter Recognition

1. Ask toddlers to find specific letters in a group of words. Using a piece of paper, write a variety of different, simple words (e.g. box, top, bed, stop, cat, bird, etc.). Then ask your toddler to circle each word that starts with a specific letter, such as the letter 'b.'

- Write a variety of these word groups and focus on different letters each time.

2. Start the letter of the day. Each day select a different letter that you and your toddler are going to

focus on. Write or display that letter somewhere prominent where your toddler will see it all day. Then ask your toddler to go through magazines or newspapers and look for words that start with the letter of the day. Get your toddler to cut that word out and post it near the letter of the day.

- Another aspect of this game is to also ask your toddler to draw an object that starts with the letter of the day. For example, if the letter of the day was 'd,' your toddler might want to draw a dog.

3. Identify letters while reading. While reading your toddler a story, ask your toddler to point out words that start with a specific letter. You could do this page-by-page to help your toddler recognize that specific letter in different words.

4. Scramble the letters of your toddler's name. In addition to simply teaching toddlers how to spell their names, you can also play a game where you scramble the letters of their name so they have to put them back in order. This works best with letter cards that can be easily mixed up and put back in order.

## How to Teach a Child to Write their Name

Teaching a child to write their name is the first step in literacy for a young child. It should be an enjoyable experience for you and the child.

## Method 1

### Using Candy

1. Get out a small white board or a piece of paper, whiteboard pens or markers, and, optionally, some candy.

2. Sit the child down at a table and sit next to him/her.

3. Tell the child that today is the day that they learn to write their name. It's okay if they can't write yet, this will give them a head start.

4. Put the paper/whiteboard and the pens/marker in front of the child.

5. First, write their name for them on the paper and explain that this is how you write their name.

6. Write their name but in little lines or spots so that they can trace them. Have them trace a few times until they get the hang of it.

7. Once their confidence grows, tell them to try it on their own.

8. They may take a while, but be patient.

- If their name is "Jack" or "Emma", this should be easy. But if their name is "Kimberly " or "Madison", this might take a while.

9. Check it to make sure they have drawn each letter correctly. Even if you see a small error like the letter "a" has it's line too long, correct the child immediately. It will be easier to correct now than later.

10. Praise the child once they have done it correct a few times. Give them them a little bit of the candy. Tell them they have earned it. Then let the child go run and play.

11. Do this for a couple days, praising the child and giving the child a little more candy every day. Soon, they will be able to write their name fluently and perfectly.

## Method 2

### Using Highlighters

Children love bright colors; highlighters can turn this learning into a lot of fun.

1. Gather highlighters of different colors, blank or lined paper, and pen or pencil.

2. Write his/her name in on solid color, switch between the different colors for each time you write the name. This will keep some interest as they complete each one.

3. Have your child trace your work with a pen or pencil.

4. Develop a reward system for your child to encourage a positive writing experience.

## Method 3

### Using Different Kinds of Letters

1. Buy some small or large (depending on the age of the child learning to write their name: small if child is over 5 and large if child is under 5) magnetic letters, a cake pan, felt letters, felt or a flannel board, and tactile letters.

2. Write the child's name on a piece of paper in pen or pencil. Tell them to copy their name with the magnetic letters. Place the magnetic letters on a cake pan with every letter.

3. Encourage the child to spell their name with the felt letters. Place the felt letters on the felt or flannel board, just like step 2. Say the letters of the child's name together after they have spelled it out.

4. Have the child spell their name with the tactile letters. The tactile letters do not have any special place to be placed but, you can lay them on a table, floor, or any clean, hard, surface. Feel the letter every time you pick a new letter up. Tell the child what the letter is unless they have learned letter recognition already. If they are trying to learn letter recognition, ask them what the letter is. If they get it right, give praise. If they get it wrong praise them for trying and tell them what the letter actually is. After the child has spelled their name, praise them and review the letters.

## How to Teach Toddlers their Colors

Do you have a toddler that keeps identifying everything around him or her as blue? Maybe you want to finally teach your toddler that there are many more fun colors in the world around him or her. But learning can be tedious for a child, so you might want to find a way to teach your toddler while having fun. By incorporating learning into fun activities and then reinforcing your lessons in everyday situations, you can teach your toddler the colors with relative ease.

### Part 1

#### Giving Fun Lessons on Colors

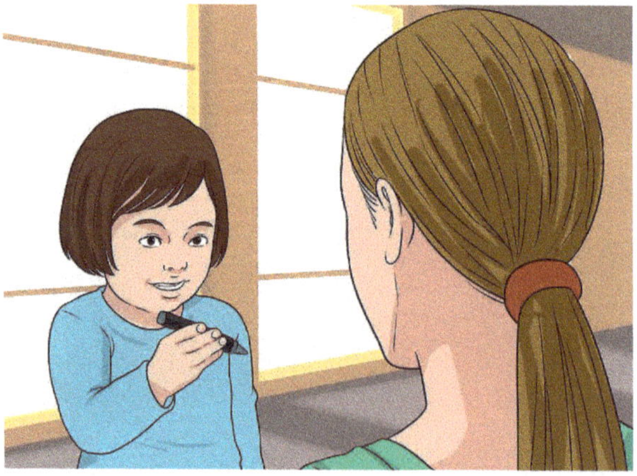

1. Use games. Children learn best when they are engaged and enjoying themselves. Using different

games and fun activities can spark your child's interest in colors and help him or her retain the information more effectively. A good way to think of this is "busy hands, busy brains."

- Try different types of games with your child and see which one he or she likes best. For example, you could ask you child to select a crayon, marker, or piece of construction that he or she likes. Then take your toddler out for a walk and say, "let's spot colors that are the same as your paper. I bet you can beat me."
- Tie a different colored ribbon to the tops of three long-handled spoons. Put them in a small pail and tell your child to dash to a specific colored spoon. Make sure to offer positive reinforcement such as, "great job, Sara, you found the pink ribbon."

2. Play dress up. Toddlers often love to pick out their own clothing and will put together all sorts of fun combinations. Use getting dressed as another opportunity to teach your little one different colors.

- Allow your toddler to pick out an item of clothing and say, "that's very nice, what color is it?" If your child knows the color, then ask him or her to get another piece of clothing in the same color. Remember to keep your color descriptions as simple as possible—no mint and green, just green.
- Let your toddler pick out all of the articles of clothing he or she wants to wear that day. As the child puts on each piece, ask him or her what color it is. If the child isn't sure, say, "this is orange, Callie, just like your favorite shirt and the oranges you love to eat."

3. Identify foods by color. Nutrition is key to helping your child grow. Because healthy foods are often bright and beautiful colors, you can use meals as a way to teach your toddler his or her colors.

- Ask your child what color a food is as you pass it to him or her. For example, say, "what color is the piece of broccoli?" If your child says, "green," give him or her a bit of positive reinforcement with a, "great job, Luca!" You can extend the lesson by asking, "what other foods are green, Luca?"
- Let your toddler pick out his or her own foods from healthy pre-selected choices. Tell your child to let you know what color each food is as he or she picks it. Make sure to reinforce the lesson as much as possible with statements like, "that's right, Emma, strawberries are red."

4. Sing a song. Songs about colors set to the tune of popular children's music can also help your toddler learn his or her colors. Teaching these songs to your child and singing them in places such as the car or the bathtub can distract your child while helping him or her to learn his colors.

- Try using "I Love Red" by Jean Warren. Sing the following to the tune of "Three Blind Mice": I love red, I love red.That's what I said, that's what I said. Firetrucks, wagons and strawberries piled high. Stop signs, hearts and pizza pies. Roses, tomatoes and apples, oh my. I love red. That's what I said.

5. Color or paint pictures together. Set aside some time every day or every couple of days to make pictures with your toddler. Most small children are thrilled to have a crayon or some finger paint with which to "draw" on a piece of paper. As you paint, ask your toddler what colors he or she is choosing and why. Then ask your toddler if he or she can tell you what colors you are using.

- Think of was to make painting or coloring a game. For example, ask your toddler, "What colors should I use today?" and let him or her run and pick out your colors for the day.

6. Compare identical objects of different colors. Introducing variables is another good way to teach your toddler colors, as well as the differences between them. Have your child compare identical objects, such as balls, of different colors. Seeing the distinction between colors can help your child more clearly identify them and their names.

- Use items you have around your house to highlight the differences. You can use things like balls, shoes, or even fish. Remember to keep the number of choices relatively low until your toddler has a good grasp on multiple colors.

## Part 2

### Using Effective Learning Tactics

1. Introduce colors gradually. Toddlers and their brains are still growing. Presenting a two or three year old child an entire box of crayons and expecting him or her to learn all of the color would overwhelm the child. Instead, have the child pick out one or two of his or her favorite colors and reinforce your lessons of those during the week. Move to a new color or two the next week and repeat this pattern until your toddler knows a wide array of colors.

- Consider starting your child with the basic colors of the rainbow. These are the ones he or she will need to know for school. Keep in mind it may also be difficult for a toddler to differentiate between similar shades of one color. It's easier for a toddler to know "red" instead of "carnelian" or "vermillion."

2. Give the object a concise description. It may be more difficult for children to learn colors in English because the name is often used before a noun—for example, "the blue whale." But by saying, "The whale is blue" instead, you can help your child successfully narrow his or her focus to the object before telling the color. In turn, this can help your toddler more quickly learn his or her colors.

3. Repeat to encourage the learning process. Repetition is important for the development of a child's brain. Stick with games and lessons your child enjoys to help him or her learn the colors more effectively and even quickly. Build on these lessons as you introduce new colors to their palette knowledge.

- Let your child use the same digital media to learn the colors. For example, make it a ritual to watch a show at the same time every day or week. Ask the same questions every week: "hey Max, you love Daniel Tiger! Can you tell me again what color he is?"

4. Reinforce lessons outside of your home. Take any opportunity you can to help your child learn

his or her colors. Playing games in the car or on walks like "I Spy" can reinforce your lessons and minimize boredom.

- Use car trips to your advantage and help your child avoid the dreaded "are we there yet?" question. As you approach traffic lights, ask your child what color is showing. You can also ask your toddler if he or she sees a certain color car.
- Have your child search for different colored foods in the grocery store.

5. Let your child show off. If you're with family or friends at gathering, give your child the chance to show off his or her new knowledge. Having the praise from others can help your toddler retain the information and motivate him or her to continuing learning the colors.

- Ask your toddler in front of others, "what color is Mrs. Neumaier's dog, Charlotte? Isn't she pretty?" Then let everyone fawn all over your toddler and how smart he or she is.
- Make sure to let your significant other know when your toddler learns his or her colors. Say to your child, "Caroline, let your mom know what color you're wearing today."

6. Reward your child. As your child begins retaining more colors or even showing off his or her knowledge, make sure to reward him or her occasionally. It doesn't need to be anything big, even a small box of crayons and coloring book or a toy will work. Tell your child, "Owen, you've been so awesome at learning your colors. Why don't you pick out a toy train that you like. What color train do you want."

## How to Teach Kids how to Draw

Teaching a child to draw is mostly a question of observing their progress and offering them new methods of exploration. For the first five years of a child's life, your teaching will be limited to providing space, time, tools, and encouragement. In later years, you may offer to teach a child new skills, such as drawing from observation, practicing perspectives, and drawing correct proportions. Avoid pushing children to change style or approach, and do not offer criticism or correction. Rather, encourage, observe, and ask open-ended questions that will help a child-artist see and imagine more details and possibilities.

### Method 1

#### Teaching 15 Month to 5 Year Olds

1. Make art part of the routine. Incorporate art-making into playtime. Make an art-zone if you want to isolate the mess. Tape down paper for them to draw on and spill on, and make a smock out of old clothes. Taping paper on a table can help a small child focus on the motion of drawing, without having to hold down and adjust the drawing paper. Buy chunky crayons and washable markers that are easy to grip.

- Children will begin their drawing by scribbling. Around 2 years of age, the scribbles will become more controlled and repetitive, and children may begin to grip crayons and markers between their thumb and pointer finger for more control.
- Offer a variety of art materials at this age. Don't focus only on drawing with tools: children can draw by tracing pictures in sand, or shaping clay and sticking it on the page. Buy washable paints, nontoxic clay, chalk, child-safe scissors, and many kinds of paper, and store in an easy to access spot.

2. Don't teach. Children develop basic motor skills with every scribble. They also develop creativity,

invention, and self-expression. A child this young needs no instructions, only appreciation. Sit with children when they draw, talk with them about their art, but do not attempt to teach.

- Avoid the impulse to correct. Small children may paint purple grass, floating people, and babies the size of houses. If you correct them you will damage their self-confidence and interrupt their natural learning progress.

3. Make observations. Rather than praising or correcting a child's art, observe it. Comment on the process, not the product. While the child draws, say "look at all the circles you are making! Some small circles are inside the big circles" or "I see you are using orange and green crayons now." Say what you like about a drawing: "that big sun makes me think of a day at the beach!" or "I like how all the trees have different colored leaves."

4. Ask open-ended questions. Avoid asking "what is it?" when presented with a drawing. Instead, ask "can you tell me about your drawing?" If a child is excited to talk about their drawing, ask more questions. A child may begin to add more details when you ask questions. When a child is drawing representational work, they will often imagine a story that goes with the work. Asking them to tell you more details of their story will encourage them to draw more details.

- If you ask "what does the girl smell," for example, they are more likely to add a nose. If you ask "is the dog lonely at night?" they may draw more animals. This kind of exchange encourages imagination, story-telling abilities, and drawing skills.

5. Make art part of emotional processing. If a child is experiencing a strong emotion, offer them paper and markers, or some clay. If a child is having a tantrum, suggest they make an angry picture. If they are sad, a sad one. Art can help children process intense emotions that may be too complex for them to put in words. Giving a child a creative activity over which they have sovereignty can help them gain a sense of control.

6. Affirm pre-writing. Around 2 ½ to 3 ½ years of age, children will begin drawing squiggles meant to represent words. These drawings are a child's first steps toward writing. As they grow, the squiggles will become more complex. A child may begin to vary short and long squiggles, or draw letter-like shapes mixed up with real letters. These drawings are an exciting sign that a child understands that words can be written to communicate meaning.

- Children are likely to tell you that certain squiggles "mean" something, or ask you to read them aloud. Affirm the meaning of the squiggles that are read to you, and ask for help reading the others.
- Let children use the texts they produce. Bring them to the post office to mail their "letters" (with an accompanying note) to relatives, Santa, or themselves.

7. Display and save their drawings. Putting children's art up is a way of letting them know their work is interesting and important. Rather than praising every individual drawing, display it. You do not have to put up every piece of art: ask each child what they would like displayed, or create a rotating "gallery" that changes weekly or monthly. Keep a portfolio of each child's drawings so they can observe their process.

- It is more important that a child's practice is affirmed than that their art products are displayed. Displaying final products is no replacement for encouraging the development of their drawing.

## Method 2

### Teaching 5 to 8 Year Olds

1. Teach your child to practice observation. Around the age of 5, you can start teaching observational drawing. This involves teaching children how to draw from the appearance of things, rather than their knowledge or imagination of them. To begin training them in observation, teach them to think of their drawings as practice. Say you are learning a new kind of drawing that takes lots of practice, and that they can practice as much as they want.

- Provide pencils and multiple pieces of paper, and gently discourage eraser use. Say they can start a drawing as many times as they want, and erase false lines when they are done.
- Do not force observational drawing on a child. Pushing a child to a new stage of drawing might discourage or stunt their learning.

- Affirm other kinds of drawings as well: storytelling and imagination based drawings, abstract or emotional drawings.

2. Train them to draw new objects. Around age 5 or 6, children develop schema, or ways of drawing things. Instead of teaching them to observe things they have "already learned" how to draw, like houses, a pet, or trees, let them pick something they have never drawn before. This will prevent them from reverting to learned habits, but will not frustrate them by requiring them to "unlearn" something they feel they have mastered.

3. Practice observing shapes. Explain that the child will be drawing an object from one side. Have the child sit where they will be when they draw, and trace your finger around the edges of the object as they are visible to the child. Then, have the child trace the edges. Next, ask the child to trace the shape in the air. They can do this with their finger and with their pencil.

4. Draw without looking down. Encourage children to draw with their eyes on the object they are drawing. Try putting a square of paper on their pencil, above the spot they grip, so that they cannot

see the line they make. Have them draw practice lines first. Have them practice drawing each part of the shape separately.

- After they have practiced the lines, let them draw the whole shape. Keep the page of practice lines nearby for further practice or reference.
- Have children practice drawing without ever looking down.
- Have children draw and only look down when they have finished drawing a line. Let them check on their progress, but encourage them to look down as little as possible.

5. Coach by observing and questioning. As you would for a younger child, ask open-ended questions, but ask them about what they see rather than what they imagine. Ask "which part of the object is lighter? Which is darker?" "where does the line bend?" Compliment lines and angles they depicted correctly, and encourage them to find more details.

- Say "I see you drew a strong curving stem for the flower, and you shaded a texture into the dirt. Now, do you see any smaller parts at the end of the stem? Where do they start and stop?"
- Avoid showing your own drawings of an object, or drawing on a child's paper. Children are hardwired to learn by imitation, but this is not helpful for learning drawing.

6. Focus on one medium at a time. Offer children the chance to practice with different media.

Children between 5-8 may be open to drawing with pencils, which will allow them to focus on shading and contour. Show children different materials and allow them to experiment. Suggest phases: first we will draw with a pencil, then with watercolors.

7. Make a book. Children between 5 and 8 enjoy making up stories to go with their drawings. They may be interested in drawing sequences to tell a longer story. Encourage children to draw and write short books. Help them bind the books together with staples or needle and thread. Once the book has been "published," put it on the bookshelf with the rest of their books.

## Method 3

### Teaching 9 to 11 Year Olds

1. Focus on spatial issues. Pre-teen children will be especially interested in depicting perspective, foreshortening, and other spatial information. They will begin to draw horizon lines, overlapping objects, and exacting detail. Assign them spatial sequences, such as drawing an object from three different angles. Arrange neutral-colored geometric shapes near one another so they can practice shading.

- Let them arrange objects in piles and draw them.

2. Teach proportion through portraiture. Basic anatomical proportion is one of the hardest things to learn. People tend to see the head as bigger than it is, the eyes as being bigger and higher in the face. Teach children basic anatomical proportions of the face, then give them mirrors and have them draw themselves. Let them take turns posing for one another, and have them draw quick sketches.

3. Anticipate the crisis of confidence. Around age 9, children have a strong desire to draw realistically. They may become frustrated by drawings that do not look "right." They may decide they are bad artist. To head off this crisis of confidence, make it clear to them that drawing is a skill that takes practice. Tell them that when they are frustrated it is because they are moving up a level. If they think they are a bad artist, that is because they have learned to see things they couldn't see before.

- Children around age 11 may wish to give up on drawing. Teaching them age-appropriate skills and encouraging them to try new methods will help them stay motivated.
- Enlarge the child's concept of art. One way to head off the decline of a child's artistic practice is to teach them other forms. Drawing abstractions, comics, or design can rekindle the confidence of a child who is stuck on realism.

4. Set them observation challenges. Children who have been observing shapes and attempting to draw realistically for a while are ready to unlearn some of the things they have learned, so long as they are not shamed for wrong answers. Bring them to a tree, or pass around pieces of wood, and explain that they are going to observe all the colors in bark. Set them the challenge of drawing a tree without using the color brown, but rather by blending different colored markers to get a real woody color.

## How to Show your Toddler Activities to Teach Colors and Shapes

Teaching toddlers can be a challenge because of the fact that toddlers are generally active little tots that have begun to think independently. As a parent or educator, you may have to rely on creative means to encourage your child to learn about colors and shapes. Luckily, there are a number of creative lessons you can use to educate your little one.

### Method 1

#### Incorporating Learning into Everyday Activities

1. Read your toddler books about colors and shapes. Books can come in very handy when trying to explain the basics of colors and shapes to your child. There are different types of books you can use

to teach these concepts, from touch and feel books, to pop-up books. Try a selection of books, or stick to the one that your child reacts to best.

- Make sure to establish routines at home when teaching these basics to your toddler. If your child pays more attention when you read to her before she goes to bed, then make it a habit to read to your child each night.

2. Connect learning with everyday activities. Make everyday an opportunity to reinforce what you have read to your toddler. Tell her "Look at your dress! Isn't it a lovely shade of RED?" or "Look at your book! It's shaped like a rectangle (or a square!)".

- Make sure to point out everyday objects to your toddler and say what shape and color they are, whether you're inside the vehicle passing by tall buildings (rectangular in shape) or walking in the park and see a balloon (oval in shape).

- Take every opportunity you have to mention the colors to your toddler and connect them with whatever activity she's doing such as "Wow! Those are really beautiful RED berries you got in your yogurt" or "Would you like to wear your pink shoes or yellow sandals"?

3. Sing nursery rhymes about shapes and colors. Nursery rhymes may help your child memorize the basic shapes and the many different hues of the color wheel.

- *Life without Colors, All in Red, What is Pink* and the ever popular ditty *Roses are Red, Violets are Blue* are just some of the nursery rhyme books you can read to your toddler about colors.

- Consider creating your own song about shapes or colors by using a familiar tune, such as "Twinkle, Twinkle Little Star" and simply making up your own words.

4. Play games about colors and shapes. Incorporate your lessons about colors and shapes into games that you make up, or games that your child is already familiar with. For example, ask your child to point out objects that are red, or find objects that are oval in shape.

- Consider playing I-Spy, with an emphasis on colors and shapes.

- When your child does well at a game, make sure to give her positive reinforcement by giving her a reward, such as some extra time to play before bed.

## Method 2

### Using Specific Learning Ideas

1. Make edible finger paints. You can whip up icing (or use a store bought variety) to make edible finger paint; simply add a few drops of food coloring to each bowl of icing so that your child has several colors to work with. Once you have several colorful icings to work with, have your child decorate cookies, or use the icing on paper. Give her an assignment, such as using only two specific colors to draw a specific thing.

- For instance, you could ask your child to make a picture of the ocean and sun, using the correct colors (blue and yellow respectively).

2. Make shapes with different colored play-doughs. You can also make homemade colorful edible play doughs. Try mixing a cup of flour with half a cup of water. Add a pinch of salt and a teaspoon of baking powder. Knead into a dough.

- If the dough is still too soft, just add a bit more flour to it until you get your desired consistency. Wrap the dough in a plastic wrap and keep it in the fridge for half an hour. Afterwards, separate the dough into as many colors as you want to use, and add a few drops of food coloring to each ball of dough. Knead the dough to incorporate the color.

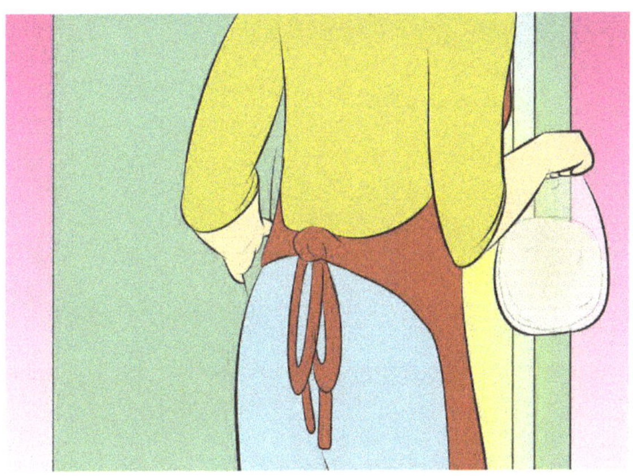

- Once your dough is ready, have your child work with the colorful dough to create shapes. Ask your child to make a purple triangle, or a blue circle.

3. Play with chalk on the sidewalk. Let your toddler scribble and doodle on the sidewalk with sidewalk chalk. Guide her drawings to help her learn her shapes and colors. Ask her to draw a scene with a pink balloon, or a yellow flower.

- You can also ask your child to draw certain shapes in different colors.

4. Use different colored jelly beans to teach colors. Place an assortment of colored jelly beans in a bowl. Give your child five or more empty cups. Ask your child to sort the jelly beans into groups of colors.

- When she does this correctly, let her reward be that she can eat one cup of the jelly beans, or one of each kind of jelly bean, depending on what she likes.

5. Test your toddler with silhouette flash cards. You can purchase these flashcards from bookstores or learning stores. Give your child the cut out shapes, and ask her to match them to the cards that have the same shapes on them. Ask her, "look at the shape you are holding; which card has the same shape on it?".

6. Encourage your toddler to sort shapes. Give your child a collection of items that are distinctly shaped like the shapes that you are trying to teach your child. Have your child sort these items into groups that are all the same shape.

- For example, give your child three balls (all in different sizes), a round plastic plate, square boxes in different sizes, a piece of paper cut into the shape of a square, and several different rectangular shoe boxes. Ask your child to sort these items into circles, squares, and rectangles.

- You can also make a batch of cookies and cut them so that there are five circles, five triangles, and five squares. Mix the cookies up and ask your child to sort them into circles, triangles and squares. As a reward, she can eat one of the cookies.

7. Feed an imaginary pet with different shaped foods. Get your child a stuffed animal, or use one that she already has. Draw images of food that have distinct shapes, such as a circular apple, or a triangle pear, and cut them out (the shapes should be exaggerated so that your child can tell the difference; the foods don't need to look like they normally do).

- Have your child feed the stuffed animal different shaped foods each day. Tell your child that today, the stuffed cat can only eat oval shaped foods.

# How to Teach your Toddler to Eat Independently

Babies eat instinctively, suckling at the breast or bottle. As they grow, they consume a much wider variety of foods, and as toddlers, they will want to eat them independently. Self-feeding takes some skill, however. You can play an important role in helping your toddler learn.

## Part 1

### Helping your Toddler Eat Finger Foods

1. Pay attention to your child's desire to self-feed. Eating with the fingers is the first way that children learn to feed themselves, and you should watch for signs that you son or daughter is ready to try. This may actually begin well before the toddler period, at around eight or nine months of age. You may notice that your older baby will try to grab food (or other items!), at first with the whole hand and then, later on, with the fingers. These are signs that he or she is ready to start learning to eat independently.

- The "pincer grasp" (the ability to grab small items with the thumb and forefinger) is especially crucial for effective self-feeding. Most babies develop this skill between about seven and eleven months of age.

2. Offer your child safe foods to eat with his or her fingers. Start by giving your older baby or younger toddler bite-sized pieces of foods that are easy to chew and swallow. At first, stick to foods that dissolve easily in the mouth; by the toddler years, you can start offering many more foods. Some suggestions include:

- low-sugar cereals, especially o-shaped and puffed varieties
- small pieces of ripe, soft fruits like bananas, mangos, peaches, or watermelon
- small pieces of soft, cooked vegetables like carrots, peas, or sweet potatoes
- cubed tofu
- cooked pasta
- small pieces of bread, bagels, or English muffins
- small bites of cheese

3. Practice with your child. Mealtimes are a chance to interact and help your child learn, so do not simply place food in front of your toddler and walk away. Sit with your child, talk about the new foods, and hold up individual bites to encourage the pincer grasp. Take your child's hand in yours and demonstrate.

4. Watch for choking. Always supervise your child when he or she is learning to eat finger foods. You can minimize the risk of choking by keeping the bites small (but not so small that he or she might swallow without chewing at all).

5. Prepare for a mess. Babies and toddlers are very messy when they learn to eat. Use bibs, and try to minimize damage by removing rugs or placing a protective cover underneath your child's high chair.

6. Praise your child's efforts. Make sure your child knows that self-feeding is a good thing and that he or she has made you proud.

## Part 2

### Teaching your Toddler to Eat with a Spoon

1. Watch for signs that your child is ready. When your older baby or younger toddler can eat finger foods and has started to grab the spoon from you during meals, he or she is probably ready to learn to eat independently with a spoon.

2. Choose the right spoon. Larger spoons will be too big for a toddler's mouth; you want something teaspoon-sized. Consider purchasing special baby spoons, which are lighter, rounded at the top, and usually made of plastic.

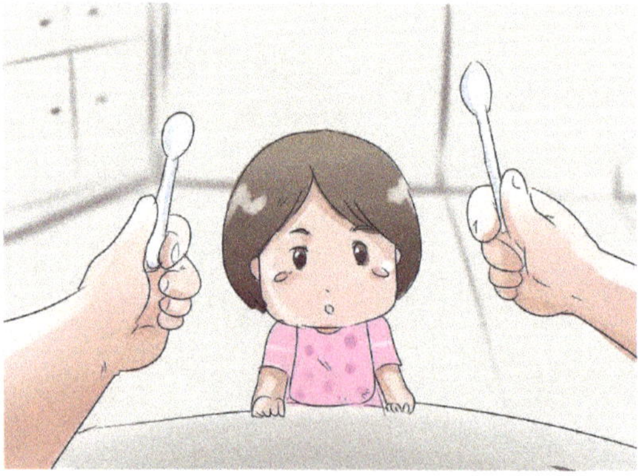

3. Start with two spoons. To begin, use two spoons: one for you and one for your child. You can feed your child as usual, and he or she can also begin trying out the spoon.

- Don't worry if, at first, your child uses the spoon primarily to bang on the plate or high chair tray and dribble food around. Self-feeding takes time; he or she will figure it out.

4. Teach your child how to use a spoon. Show your toddler how to hold a spoon, and then help by placing your hand over his or her hand to demonstrate. Direct the spoon slowly into your toddler's mouth.

- As your toddler learns, you can also start using two bowls. You can feed your child from one; he or she can use the other, which should just have a small amount of food in it.

5. Pick foods strategically. Start with thicker, denser foods; these will stay on the spoon, whereas more liquid foods will drip away before your child manages to get the spoon to his or her mouth. Yogurt, cottage cheese, and pudding work well. As your child progresses, move on to thinner purees and soups.

6. Set an example. Eat when your child eats; family meals are important for teaching self-feeding skills, communication, and manners.

7. Praise your child's efforts. Let your toddler know you are proud of his or her growing independence.

## Part 3

### Teaching your Toddler to Eat with a Fork

1. Wait until your toddler is ready. In general, it's best to wait until your son or daughter has developed a strong pincer grasp and can use the spoon relatively well. At that point, you can introduce the fork. Most children are ready by fifteen to eighteen months or so.

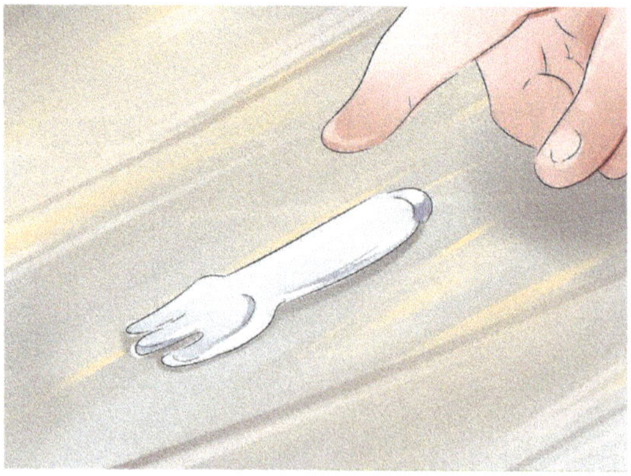

2. Choose the right fork. To begin, select a fork made for young children, with rounded tips and a lighter weight. These are both safer and easier for a toddler to use successfully.

3. Start with foods that are easy to pierce. Offer larger pieces of food that are fairly easy to pierce and hold with a fork: cubes of cheese work well, as do some kinds of cooked vegetables, meats, and pastas. Avoid foods that are too small, crumbly, or slippery. You don't want to frustrate your child unnecessarily.

4. Help your child use the fork. In the beginning, you may need to take your child's hand and demonstrate how to pierce and pick up a piece of food.

5. Encourage eating with the fork. Once your toddler is two or so, it's fine to encourage fork-eating, but don't worry if your child continues to prefer using his or her fingers. You can wait until the preschool years to start pushing harder for better table manners.

6. Praise your child's efforts. Again, let your toddler know that you are impressed with his or her new skills.

## Part 4

### Helping your Toddler Drink Independently

1. Let babies drink independently from a bottle. Before the toddler years, you can let an older baby hold a bottle and drink on his or her own. This will prepare your child for using a cup later on.

2. Introduce a cup with a lid. Most children can start to drink from a cup by about a year of age.

Make life easier for both of you by starting with a lidded cup made for toddlers. This will minimize spills and mimic the "feel" of a bottle.

- Understand that even with a lidded cup, your child will probably make a mess. That's okay; it's part of the learning process.

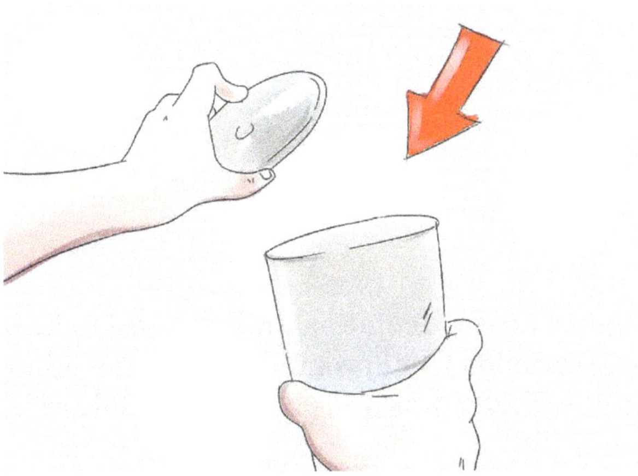

3. Remove the lid. Once your child has mastered drinking from a lidded cup, you can remove the lid. Don't fill the cup more than halfway – better to refill multiple times than to have your child dump a completely full cup all over the place.

4. Help your toddler as necessary. You can ease your child into drinking from a cup by holding the cup steady during his or her first attempts, placing your hands over your toddler's hands so that he or she gets the sense of what drinking from a cup should feel like.

## How to Teach your Toddler to Sit Still

Toddlers are typically energetic and easily distracted, and they get fidgety, cranky, and uncomfortable when they are required to sit still and behave themselves. This is totally normal, and you shouldn't worry if it seems that your toddler has something along the lines of a one-minute attention span. Still, there are times when you'll need to get your toddler to sit still.

## Part 1

### Developing the Ability to Sit Still

1. Practice sitting still. Sitting still does not come naturally to most toddlers, but you can practice the skill at home. To start, have your toddler sit in your lap for one full minute. Challenge your child to sit as still as possible. Gradually lengthen the time until your child can sit still for longer stretches.

- Do not entertain your toddler too much during these practice sessions. Playing, tickling, singing, and the like defeat the purpose: you're trying to get your child to tolerate peaceful stretches of time without entertainment.
- As your toddler improves at this exercise, you can switch from your lap to a chair. Sit next to your child and continue to challenge him to sit still.

2. Read aloud to your child. Reading aloud engages your toddler in a quiet, attentive activity, building his or her ability to focus and sit peacefully. Teach your toddler to pay attention to details: ask questions and point out interesting things in the pictures.

3. Encourage artistic activities. Make sure your toddler has access to paper, crayons, pencils, and/

or paint. These activities are also engaging and encourage a longer attention span. Challenge your child to finish a picture before moving on to something else.

- At first, it may help to participate in these activities alongside your child. Having your attention may encourage your child to focus on an artistic endeavor for a longer period of time. As he or she learns to be more focused and attentive, you can begin to sit back and watch.

4. Play games that require quiet attention. Try to get your toddler to play with blocks, puzzles, and other games that don't involve physical activity. These games help toddlers develop memory skills, fine motor coordination, and the ability to sit still.

5. Build quiet moments into your family's routines. Choose some regular times to sit quietly together as a family, perhaps at the beginning of a meal or at some designated time for quiet reading. If your toddler sees his or her parents and siblings modeling appropriate activity, he or she will catch on more quickly.

6. Use mealtimes as practice. Young children should learn to sit quietly at the table during meals.

Make sure your child understands that running around during meals is unacceptable; he or she needs to sit still and finish eating before getting up to play. Because mealtimes occur so regularly, they offer a great opportunity for practicing your toddler's skills.

- Set a good example during mealtimes. When you sit down to dinner with your family, do not get up to answer the phone or see what's on television.
- Consider letting your child bring a doll or teddy bear to the table as a dining companion. Point out that the doll or teddy does not jump around at the table.

7. Reward your child's efforts. When your toddler does a good job sitting still or paying attention, offer lots of specific praise. Consider offering a small treat – a piece of chocolate, a trip to the park – for particularly good behavior.

## Part 2

### Helping your Child Sit Still

1. Prepare your child. If you are going to be in a situation where your toddler will have to sit still, start preparing early. Let your toddler know what the situation will be and what kind of behavior you expect. Typical situations include:

- Restaurant meals. Even more than meals eaten at home, meals eaten at restaurants demand good behavior. Don't expect miracles – choose family-friendly restaurants – but let your toddler know that he or she needs to sit still and behave.

- Haircuts. If your toddler wiggles, fidgets, and jumps around, it will be very difficult to manage a good haircut. Explain this to your child in advance, and suggest that he or she sit as still as possible and watch the haircut in the mirror.
- Medical examinations. Children do need to sit still during medical exams, especially for blood tests and other lab work. Prepare your child in advance. During the exam, try to occupy your child as best you can. Distract by pointing out colorful paintings or drawings, and use your imagination: a drop of blood can be a ladybug or raspberry juice.
- Church, concerts, and theater performances. Again, prepare your child in advance. Understand, though, that your child may not be able to sit still for something as lengthy as a church service or a concert. Plan to take quick breaks, taking your child outside to burn off some energy.

2. Make sure your child's basic needs are met. You cannot expect a hungry, thirsty, exhausted, or otherwise uncomfortable toddler to sit still and behave; it will not happen. Don't attempt any event that requires sitting still without feeding your toddler and making sure his or her other needs are met.

3. Distract your child. When your child needs to sit still, whether it's during a meal or at a doctor's appointment, it helps to offer a distraction. Have your child focus on a painting on the wall, his or her image in the mirror, a silly song or story – anything that works. If necessary, bring favorite toys, picture books, and snacks.

- In rare cases, you may want to break out a cartoon or electronic device. This can work when you really need your child to stay still – as at the doctor's office or barber shop. But don't use this strategy very often; you'll only teach your child to zone out in front of a screen.

4. Dress your child to suit the activity. When your toddler is running around, you can dress him or her in play clothes and sneakers. When you are doing something that will require "best behavior," change clothing to reflect your expectations. Teach your child to recognize the difference.

- Do not, however, dress your child in anything too stiff, uncomfortable, or confining. This could backfire, making your child more fidgety than ever.

5. Be an authority figure. Children have the right to play and enjoy a carefree childhood, but you still have to keep things under control. Remember that you set the rules, and you need to expect your toddler to respect them.

- At the same time, keep your expectations in check. Don't punish a toddler for failing to sit quietly through an hour-long church service; that's not fair. But do consider mild, age-appropriate punishments for bad behavior.

6. Give your child choices. Although you are the authority, you can still give your child some

control. Let your toddler make some decisions. Will he or she sit in your lap or in a chair? Does he or she want apple slices or cheese cubes? Permitting your toddler to make some choices will allow a sense of independence and control.

7. Praise good behavior. Let your toddler know that you are proud when he or she sits quietly and behaves well.

## How to Potty Train your Child

The prospect of potty training can be daunting - for both you and your child! The main thing you need to consider is whether your child is ready to be potty trained - if they are, then the whole process will be a lot easier, not to mention faster. Read below to find out how to go about potting training your child - with advice on everything from how to know if your child is ready, to setting up an effective potty-training schedule, to praising your child's successes and offering appropriate rewards. Ready, steady, potty!

### Part 1

#### Preparing to Potty Train

1. Know when your child is ready. It is very important that your child is developmentally ready to learn how to use the potty, as this will make the process so much easier and faster. When a child

is ready to be potty trained will vary from child to child, and can be any age from 18 to 36 months. In general, girls tend to be toilet trained slightly earlier than boys - the average age for girls is 29 months, whereas for boys it's 31.

- You can tell if your child is ready to potty train by looking out for the following signs:
    - ◊ Showing an interest in the bathroom and how other people use it.
    - ◊ Possessing good motor skills - including the ability to walk to the bathroom, climb steps and pull down pants.
    - ◊ Using language skills - being able to understand simple instructions and follow them.
    - ◊ Having predictable bowel movements.
    - ◊ Understanding - through words or facial expression - of when they need to urinate or have a bowel movement.
    - ◊ Wanting to please parents and act like a grown up.
    - ◊ Knowing what the words wet and dry, clean and dirty, and up and down mean.
    - ◊ Keeping their diaper dry for two hours and waking up dry from a nap occasionally.
    - ◊ Wanting to get out of diapers and into underwear or training pants, and asking to get out of that dirty diaper.
    - ◊ Becoming more interested in being clean and dry. Noticing sticky fingers, dirty feet an diapers, etc.
- You should never push your child to potty train if they are not ready - they will only resist you and the potty training process will be frustrating and time-consuming. Give you child another month or two and you will find it much easier.
- It has also been proved that one of the most effective ways to potty train, is to start the process way before the physical process starts, with games and activities to prepare them for the general idea.

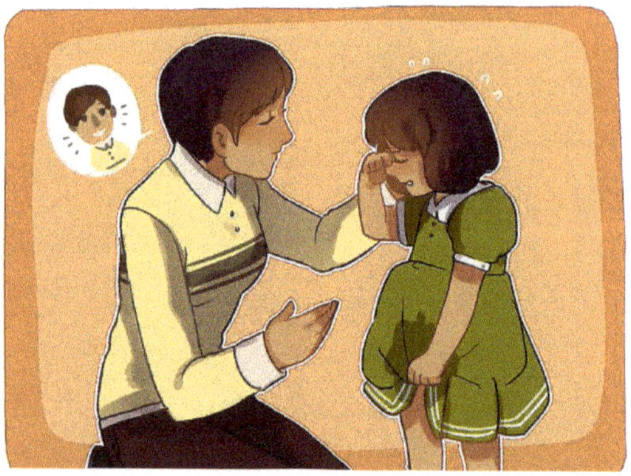

2. Understand that the potty training process will take time. The number one thing you need in order to successfully potty train your child is patience! Potty training is a process, it does not happen overnight. You and your child will need to work on it together and overcome any accidents and

setbacks. Although you hear of some parents who potty train their child over the course of a single weekend, it is completely normal for the training process to take up to six months.

- Try to be as consistently upbeat and encouraging with your child as possible and deal with any accidents calmly. Remember that no child is going to graduate high school in diapers - they *will* get there.
- You should also be aware that although your child might be fully potty trained during the day, it is common for children to continue wetting the bed at night until the age of five. They should be able to stay completely dry by the age of six, but until that time be prepared to use pull-ups and plastic sheets at night.

3. Get the right equipment. A training potty is the easiest and least intimidating option for a child new to potty training. You can get all sorts of cute potties, some in the shape of your child's favorite cartoon characters. These are a good choice as you want your child to feel as comfortable as possible with the potty and enthusiastic about using it. You should also consider getting a potty with a removable seat, which you can place on the toilet once your child is ready.

- If you decide to use the toilet from the beginning, make sure to get a step stool for your child so their feet feel firm and secure while sitting on it. This will make them feel more stable and help eliminate the fear of falling in.
- Consider placing the potty in the playroom or living area to begin with. This will help your child to get comfortable with the potty and less intimidated by the prospect of using it. They may also be more inclined to use it if it's within easy reach.

4. Choose the right time. Choosing the right time to potty train can make a huge difference in your chance of success. Avoid trying to potty train if your child has recently gone through a period of

change - such as the arrival of a new sibling, moving to a new house or starting at a new day care - as these things can be stressful for a child and potty training will only add to that stress.

- Choose a period when you can spend long periods of time with your child at home - so they will feel comfortable and secure with their environment and always have you there for encouragement and support.
- Many parents choose to potty train their children over the summer months - not only because they tend to have more free time to spend with their children, but also because their child will be wearing less layers of clothing, which makes getting to the potty on time much easier for the child.

5. Set a schedule. Setting a schedule can help turn potty time into a routine, which will help your child adjust to their new responsibility and help them to remember to go all by themselves. To start off, try picking two to three times a day when you will put your child on the potty and let them sit there for a few minutes. If they use it, that's great, but if not don't worry about. You just need your child to get used to the feel of it.

- To encourage your child to go, try to pick times when he/she is most likely to need the bathroom, like first thing in the morning, after mealtimes and before bed. You can also give your child extra liquids with their meals if you like, as this will help to get their digestive system going.
- Make potty time part of your child's bedtime routine - they put their pajamas on, wash their face, brush their teeth and go to the potty. They'll soon remember to go all by themselves.

## Part 2

### Getting your Child Comfortable with the Potty

1. Introduce your child to the potty. Let your child get comfortable with it, so they understand that

the potty is not an intimidating or scary thing at all. Put the potty in their play area, where they can sit on it fully clothed, while reading a book or playing with toys. Once they've grown accustomed to or even fond of the potty, you can move it to the bathroom.

2. Show your child how to use it. Your child next needs to understand what the potty is actually *for*. To explain it, try taking your child's dirty nappy and popping its contents into the potty. Tell them the potty is where the "poop" and "pee-pee" goes. Alternatively, you can put the contents of the nappy in the toilet and let them wave goodbye as it flushes away.

- You can also demonstrate how the toilet is used by bringing the child into the bathroom with you when you need to go. Have them sit on the potty as you sit on the toilet and show them how it's done. With any luck, this will encourage them to use the potty like a "big boy" or "big girl".
- If possible, little boys might be better off going to the bathroom with Daddy, to avoid being! However, you should forget about teaching boys to pee standing up just yet, as this can be confusing for them (not to mention messy). For now, have them sit on the potty for number ones as well as number twos.

3. Let your child sit on the potty for at least 15 minutes a day. Let your child get accustomed to the potty by letting them sit on it for five minutes, three times a day. Encourage them to go, but don't worry if they don't. Praise them for trying and let them know that they can try again later.

- If they're impatient to get off, try reaching into that potty basket for some entertainment.
- To create a potty basket or box, find a small box or basket that is at least one foot (12 inches) long, and half a foot (6 inches) wide. Borrow 2-3 potty books from your local library to place in the potty basket/box. An electronic device with potty apps, movies, videos, and songs on it will also entertain, although the use of this should be limited to one hour a day. Make sure that your child's drink-and-wet doll with a cup and possibly a potty of his/her own is in the basket: your child can make the doll "go" in the toilet and can make them feel proud of "teaching" their doll to use the toilet. A few extra pairs of underwear or training pants is helpful in case of accidents and a pack of flushable wipes is great for your child to wipe better and helps give a better clean after accidents. A sippy cup of water will help your child go and a coloring picture on a clipboard with crayons attached makes for even more entertainment. Of course, paper towels are helpful for cleaning up messes, and potty flashcards can be lifesavers.
- Never force your child to sit on the potty if they don't want to - you'll only cause further resistance which can upset the whole training process.

4. Use the right toilet-related words. Try not to confuse your child by using vague or obscure words to describe the act of using the toilet or the names of particular body parts. Use easy, straight-forward, child-friendly words like "pee", "poop" and "potty" when speaking to your child.

- Never use words like "dirty" or "disgusting" to describe natural bodily processes, as this can cause your child to feel ashamed or embarrassed about their actions, which can negatively-impact the potty training process.
- If a child feels anxious or embarrassed about using the potty, they can start to hold everything in - which can lead to health problems such as constipation and urinary tract infections. For this reason, it is very important that a child feels comfortable with using the potty.
- Being open with your child will give them confidence and let them know that they should feel proud of themselves for using the potty correctly.

5. Stay with your child while they use the potty. Children can feel extremely anxious about using the potty for a variety of reasons - if they are using the toilet they can be afraid of falling in or scared of the flushing noise that the toilet makes. Other children may see their bowel movements as part of themselves, which they feel they are losing by using the potty. For this reason, it is important that you stay with your child at all times while they are on the potty, at least at first.

- Smile at your child, give plenty of praise, and use a calm, soothing tone of voice at all times. You can also try singing songs or playing games with your child while they're on the potty, so they come to see potty-time as a fun activity, rather than something to be feared.

6. Read potty-themed picture books. Many parents have found books dealing with the subject of potty training to be an extremely helpful tool in teaching their child how and why they should use the potty. These books are often humorous and encouraging, with engaging pictures which children can relate to.

- Get your child involved in the reading process by asking questions and getting your child to point out certain items in the pictures. Then once you've finished reading, ask your child if they'd like to try using their potty, just like the little boy or girl in the book.

- Some popular potty-related books include "Once Upon A Potty" by Alona Frankel, "Everyone Poops" by Taro Gomi, and "I Want My Potty" by Tony Ross.

## Part 3

### Creating Good Habits

1. Learn your child's "need-to-go" signals. If you can learn to read the signs that your child needs to use the bathroom, then you can get them to the bathroom quickly and encourage them to use the potty instead of going in their diaper.

- Common signals that a child needs to use the bathroom include: a change or pause in activity; squatting; clutching at their diaper; grunting; turning red in the face.
- You can help your child to recognize these signs themselves by asking them "Do you need to use the potty?" or "Do you need to poop?" as soon as you notice the warning signs. Encourage your child to tell you whenever they feel like they need to go.
- Be aware that some children will be reluctant to stop what they're doing, especially if they are playing and having fun, just to use the potty. You will need to encourage them and give them lots of praise to make it seem worth their while.

2. Let your child go nappy-free for an hour or two a day. Many parents recommend the technique of removing a child's diaper and letting them run around the house naked for a couple of hours a day. They will enjoy the feeling, while also learning to recognize their body's "need-to-go" signals, without the safety net of a diaper.

- Be aware that you will have accidents if you decide to employ this method - but an accident (or five) may be just what your child needs to realize the importance of using the potty!
- Don't act cross or disappointed when your child has an accident - just clean it up calmly and reassure your child that they'll make it to the potty on time next time. If you scold them, they may become anxious about using the potty and start holding.
- Many parents dislike using pull-up diapers because they are now so absorbent that a child cannot tell if it is wet or not. Without some feeling of discomfort, they will not be able to learn their body's signals and make it to the bathroom on time. If the child is naked, or wearing cloth underwear however, there will be no mistaking the need to go.

3. Make using the potty part of the morning or nighttime routine. Using the potty needs to become a normal and natural daily activity for your child, and the best way to make this happen is to incorporate potty time into their pre-existing daily routine.

- Sit them on the potty after they brush their teeth each morning, or before their nightly bath. Do this every day and night, without fail, and your child will soon be hopping on the potty all by themselves.

4. Show your child how to wipe correctly and flush the toilet. Instruct your child on how to wipe themselves properly with toilet paper before they hop off the potty. Make it easier for them by

always leaving a roll of toilet paper (maybe the decorated kind!) beside the potty. This is particularly important for girls in particular, who should wipe from front to back to avoid spreading bacteria.

- They will probably still need help wiping for some time, especially after a number two, but is good to get your child into the habit of trying.
- Once they are done, let your child do the honors of flushing the toilet and wave goodbye or cheer as everything gets flushed away. Congratulate your child on a job well done!

5. Remind your child to wash their hands after they use the potty. Children are usually impatient to get back to the important business of playtime once they are finished with the potty, but you must make sure to emphasize how important it is for your child to wash their hands before leaving the bathroom.

- To encourage hand washing, get your child a step stool so they can easily reach the sink and buy some children's anti-bacterial soap in a bright color that they will enjoy using.
- Teach your child to sing a song while they wash, so they will not be tempted to wash too quickly. Get them to sing the alphabet when they start washing their hands and tell them they can only stop when they get to the letter Z!

## Part 4

### Dealing with Successes and Setbacks

1. Praise your child for trying. The most important thing you can do for your child during potty

training is to offer endless encouragement, regardless of whether they succeed in using the potty or not. Praise them for every little success - from telling you when they need to go, to pulling down their own pants, to sitting on the toilet for a full minute. Even if they don't end up going, tell your child well done for trying and remind them that they can try again later.

- Just be careful not to *over*-encourage your child. Offer praise in a calm voice and don't get over-excited. Being too over-the-top with your encouragement is it's own form of pressure and may cause your child to feel anxious about pleasing you.

2. Offer rewards for small successes. Many children respond well to incentives or rewards for using the potty. What kind of rewards you decide to offer will depend on both your parenting style and what your child responds to. Some ideas are outlined below.

- Food: Some parents use candy as a reward for successfully using the potty. For instance, you could give your child three mini M&M's or a jelly worm every time they manage to go in the potty. Other parents are wary of offering food as a reward, as they believe it might affect their children's eating habits in future.
- Star Charts: Another common in motivator is for parents to create a star chart, where a child is given an additional gold star for every time they successfully use the potty. Sometimes the gold star is motivation enough in itself, while other times parents offer additional rewards if a child reaches a certain number of stars by the end of the week - such as a trip to the park or an extra story at bedtime.
- Toys: Another good option is to buy a small set of toys (nothing big - maybe just a collection of toy cars or plastic animals) and let your child choose one every time they use the potty.
- Piggy Bank: Some parents offer their children monetary incentives to use the potty! Put a piggy bank in the bathroom and pop a penny in every time your child uses the potty. Once it's full your child can cash it in to buy some treats, like an ice cream or a ride on the machines at the mall.

3. Share the good news. A great way to encourage your child to take pride in using the potty, is to let them boast about it to a friend or family member. Make a big deal of them being able to tell Mommy or Daddy about how well they did with the potty when he or she comes home at the end of the day. Or else give grandma or Uncle Joe a heads up and let your child ring them to tell them the good news.

- Getting positive, encouraging reactions from someone other than you (the potty trainer) will impress upon your child how good it feels to "be a big boy/girl."
- Another trick parents use is to rope in a friend or family member to portray their child's hero or favorite cartoon character over the phone. It could be Dora the Explorer, Spider-man or Barney the Dinosaur - whoever your child likes. Telling their hero about their potty training successes and getting praised in return will make them feel proud as punch.

4. Don't scold your child when they have an accident. Scolding and giving punishments are major no-nos when it comes to potty training. Remember that your child has only recently developed the ability to recognize and control their bladder and bowel movements, and they are still getting the hang of things. They don't intentionally have accidents just to annoy you or cause you extra work.

- As mentioned before, scolding a child for having an accident or failing to use the potty can cause them to develop anxiety around the whole issue. This anxiety may cause them to start trying to hold everything in, which just causes further accidents and may lead to both health and psychological problems done the line.

- If your child has an accident reassure them that it's okay and that they will make it to the potty next time round. Let them know that you're proud of them for trying and that you're confident that they will soon be using the potty just like a big boy or girl.

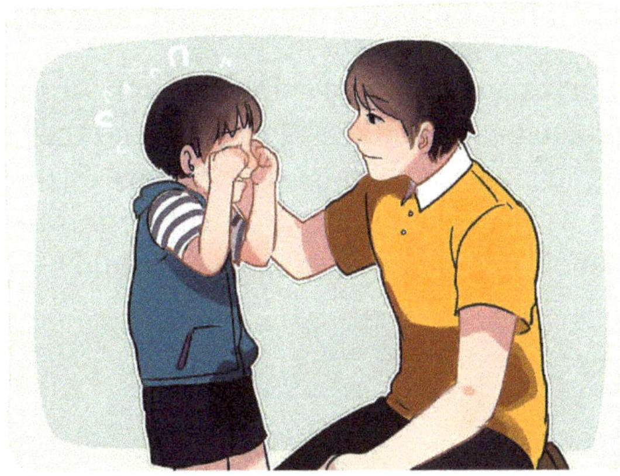

5. Have patience. Potty training can be a stressful and frustrating time for parents, but remember that it is only temporary and your child *will* get the hang of it sooner or later. Don't start panicking about whether your child has development issues if things aren't going well. When your child is ready, they'll pick it up just fine.

- If your child just doesn't seem to be getting the hang of it, the best thing to do might be to give potty training a break for a month or two and then try again.
- Remember, some kids don't become fully potty trained until they're three - and that's perfectly normal.

## Part 5

### Taking Potty Training to the Next Level

1. Let your child pick out some "big boy" or "big girl" underwear. Once your child is doing well and using the potty consistently you can bring them shopping to pick out some "big boy underpants" or "big girl underwear" together. They will feel so proud and grown up wearing them, it will make you smile! Let them wear the underwear at home, though you may want to continue using diapers or training pants at night or when you're on the go, as accidents *will* happen.

- Cloth underwear will actually help your child with their training, as they will be able to tell when the underwear are wet - something which is not so easy with absorbent diapers.
- They will also be so pleased with their new underwear that they will be reluctant to get them wet, and therefore more diligent about keeping them dry.

2. Take the potty on the road. Getting the hang of using the potty or toilet at home is one thing, but strange, unfamiliar bathrooms can be intimidating to a child and they may refuse to use them. You can overcome this, and avoid putting your child back in diapers if you're trying to phase them out, by bringing the potty with you while travelling. Potties with removable seats are great for this, as you can pop them onto the seat of any toilet to recreate your child's comfort zone.

3. Teach your boy to pee standing up. Once your little boy has got the hang of peeing sitting down, it's time for him to master the art of doing it while standing up. Daddy can help with this one, by showing his little man how it's done. Just be aware that little boy's aim is not usually the greatest and you can expect some interesting attempts at making it into the bowl.

- One great method some parents use for training their boys how to get their pee in the bowl is to put some Cheerios or Fruit Loops in the toilet bowl and tell their son to aim directly for them. This turns it into a fun game which appeals to most boys' mischievous side.

4. Let babysitters and teachers know. Your potty training efforts will be undermined if your child is not being encouraged to use the potty by babysitters or child minders. Take the time to talk to

anybody who frequently cares for your child - whether it's grandparents or the employees at your child's day care - and politely explain how important it is that they keep up your child's potty routine.

- Tell them about your child's normal schedule, along with the words you use to refer to any potty-related activities, and ask them to follow the same lines. This will prevent your child from becoming confused and your potty-training routine from being disrupted.
- Always send a spare change of clothes, some wipes, and a few emergency diapers or training pants with your child whenever they are away from home. This will make things easier on the caregivers and help your child to feel less embarrassed about any accidents.

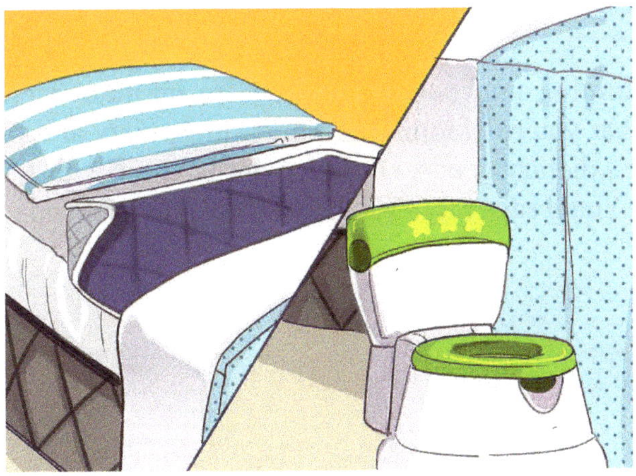

5. When your child is ready, progress to night training. When they are dry or fairly dry most days, your child may be ready for nap and night-training. If so, invest in some bed pads (you'll want at least 3 so you can change them easily) and put one on top of the bottom sheet on your child's bed. Look for the kind that have a soft layer on top and a plastic layer underneath. When that's done, put the potty next to the bed when your child goes to bed or goes for a nap.

- Leave your child's bedroom door open and encourage them to call you if they wake up needing to go. If they do, put them quickly on the potty and praise them for doing so well.
- If they go in the bed, change the pad and don't make a big deal of it. Deal with it calmly and matter-of-factly and reassure your child that it's okay. Remember that children may reach the age of six before they stop having accidents at night-time.

# Planning Meals at a Day Care 5

Children require a different diet as compared to adults. Their nutritional needs and metabolism are unique. Hence, children at a day care must be provided with specially prepared, clean and hygienic food. The aspects elucidated in this chapter are of vital importance and provide a better understanding of food and nutrition at child day care.

## How to Consider the Factors when Planning Meals

When you're choosing, planning and cooking meals, there are many factors to consider. You want to make sure the meals that you're planning are nutritious, tasty and budget-friendly while also accommodating everyone's dietary needs. Once you get familiar with the factors, planning meals in advance will be a snap. You'll save money, eat healthily and save time, as well.

### Method 1

#### Addressing Dietary Requirements

1. Include a variety of foods from the major food groups. A balanced diet requires eating a variety of fruits, vegetables, whole grains, low-fat dairy products, and lean protein (this includes beans and other legumes, nuts and seeds). Most of the foods you eat every day should fit into one of these categories.

- Try to make plant-derived foods such as whole grains, vegetables and fruits the foundation of every meal.
- After establishing a basis of plant-derived foods for a meal, then add in a moderate amount of low-fat dairy and lean protein items.

2. Use a variety of ingredients, flavors and textures. Since calories, nutrients and fiber content of foods in the same food group can differ dramatically, good nutrition depends on getting a variety of different foods from within the food groups.

- Mix up it by using an assortment of colors, shapes, flavors and textures.
- The diversity in your choices will also make meals more interesting and appealing for everyone.

3. Take proper portion sizes into account. When people are faced with overly large portions, they tend to overeat. Check the packages of foods you're preparing to about serving sizes and follow the guidelines. Unless you intend to make a lot of food so that there will be leftovers, try to follow basic serving size guidelines.

- One serving of meat or fish is approximately 3 ounces.
- One serving of dairy is approximately 1 cup.
- One serving of vegetables is approximately 1 cup raw and ½ cup cooked.
- One serving of whole grains is 1 slice of bread, 1 cup of dry cereal, and ½ cup cooked rice, cereal and pasta.
- One serving of fruit is 1 medium sized fresh piece (approximately the size of a baseball) and ¼ cup dried.

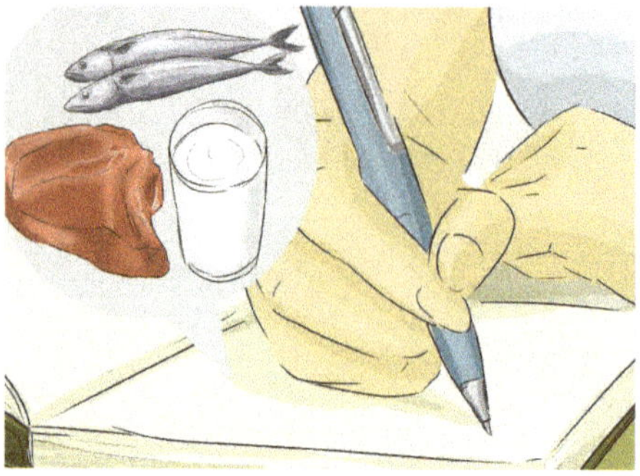

4. Avoid foods that are very high in fat, sugar, calories and sodium. While they can't be eliminated completely, a healthy, balanced diet includes a very low percentage of these types of foods. Our bodies need fat, but try to mostly choose healthy fats for your meals.

- A few healthy fat options are avocados, salmon, albacore tuna, nuts and peanut butter.

5. Address the dietary needs of different age groups. Teenagers and adults over the age of 50 need a lot of calcium in their diets. Small children, adolescent girls, and women of childbearing age need plenty of iron, which you can get from lean meats and cereals (with added nutrients).

- Women trying to become pregnant need extra folic acid.
- Elderly adults need to take in extra vitamin D.

## Method 2

### Accommodating Lifestyle and Allergy Concerns

1. Find out if anyone is vegetarian or vegan. Vegetarians do not eat meat, poultry, or seafood. Some

vegetarians don't eat dairy, so make sure to get the details from them if you're feeding a vegetarian. Vegans don't eat meat, poultry, or seafood, or any other animal products (including milk and eggs).

- Since their diets are somewhat restricted, vegans and vegetarians need a lot of variety in their food choices in order to meet their nutrition needs.
- Some food options that are popular among vegetarians and vegans are kale, grains, nuts, legumes, and beans.

2. Inquire about food allergies and intolerances. Some people have negative, sometimes even life-threatening, reactions to specific kinds of foods, so make sure to ask about them. The Mayo Clinic names eggs, milk, peanuts, shellfish, tree nuts, soy and fish as some of the most common food allergens. Wheat is another big one.

- Common food intolerances are lactose (which is in milk products), MSG and gluten (which is in bread, pasta, and many wheat products).

3. Find out if anyone is on a special diet for other health reasons. People with heart disease, high cholesterol levels and high blood pressure need to avoid certain foods to maintain good health. Some of the major foods they should avoid are processed meats, highly refined and processed carbohydrates, and sodas and other types of sugary drinks.

- Diabetics also need to avoid certain foods to maintain proper insulin levels, so be sure to ask about this one, too.

4. Inquire about religion-related food restrictions. Some people don't eat certain foods because of their religion. There are many different types of religions with food restrictions, and the restrictions themselves vary from religion to religion.

- Some religions have food restrictions only at certain times of the year, so be sure to ask about the details.

## Method 3

### Sticking to a Budget

1. Plan ahead. The best way to stick to a budget is to plan your meals one week in advance. Decide which meals you want to make for the upcoming week and make a detailed grocery list of needed ingredients.

- Be sure to take the list with you when you go shopping, so that you'll only pick up the items that you need.

2. Check out current grocery store sales. As you're planning your meals, take into account which

food products are on sale and where, and do your shopping at those places. By sticking to your shopping list and creating planned meals around sales, you can save even more money.

- Don't forget to check the newspaper for coupons and additional ways to save.

3. Use seasonal fruits and vegetables. Not only will seasonal fruits and veggies be easier to find, they will also be available in abundance for a much lower price than usual. When they're in season, fruits and veggies tend to be at their tastiest, making them ideal foods to stock up on.

- When fruit and vegetables aren't in season, buy canned or frozen varieties, which are generally cheaper while still offering great nutritional benefits.
- Along with your local grocery stores' produce section, also check out any farmer's markets in your area for even more options and organic produce at a low price.

4. Incorporate foods that you already have and buy low-cost items. Check out what's currently in your pantry. For instance, do you have some canned food items pushed to the very back of your pantry that have been in there awhile? Plan a few meals around those.

- According to the USDA, the least-expensive vegetables are eggplants, lettuce, carrots and tomatillos.
- The least-expensive fruits are apples, peaches, pineapples, pears, bananas and watermelon.
- For low-cost sources of protein, opt for canned tuna, ground beef and eggs.

## Method 4

### Checking Availability of Ingredients and Resources

1. Plan according to how much time you have to cook. Take into account how much time you have each day to cook. For instance, if you work 8 or more hours per day, you're going to have less time available for preparing meals. Plan meals that are faster and easier to prepare.

- Invest in a crock pot. You do a quick prep the night before, toss everything in the crock pot the next morning, turn it on and you're done! When you arrive back home later that evening, your meal will be waiting for you.
- Cook large batches and freeze portions for later meals.
- Use canned items, like beans, for a quicker meal prep. No hours of soaking required.
- When you're short on time, use frozen vegetables instead of fresh. Frozen veggies are still nutritious, and you'll save tons of prep time.
- Explore new recipes that incorporate baking, grilling and sauteing. Baking casseroles, for example, generally requires a short prep time and once you pop it in the oven, you don't have to babysit it.

2. Make sure you have the right equipment. Be certain that you have the cookware, utensils, dishes and other items required for the meals you're planning on hand before you buy all of the ingredients

to make them. If you are planning large meals with the intention of having leftovers, make sure you have enough storage containers and Tupperware to accommodate everything.

3. Confirm that the ingredients can be easily attained. Avoid recipes that require fruits and vegetables that are out of season. Also avoid recipes that require gourmet ingredients or any other hard-to-find items.

- If you're planning large meals, make sure the ingredients you need can be easily obtained in large quantities.

4. Avoid elaborate food preparation unless you have help. If you're cooking alone, don't plan elaborate or complex meals that require a lot of preparation. Plan meals that you can easily handle yourself, unless you have people around in your house that can assist you.

## How to make Homemade Baby Food

When it is time to introduce solids to your child (when they are between 4 and 6 months old) it's comforting to know exactly what they'll be eating. Making your own baby food at home allows you to keep track of every single ingredient in your baby's newly expanding diet. You don't need a lot of fancy gear to make homemade baby food. With a few pieces of equipment, some fresh produce and the following guidelines, you can prepare a nutritious meal or snack for your baby.

## Part 1

### Preparing Homemade Baby Food

1. Select fresh, good-quality produce. The first step in producing tasty, nutritious food for your baby is to select fresh, good quality produce.

- Buy organic if possible, and make sure fruits and vegetables are ripe and blemish-free. Try to use or cook all foods within 2 or 3 days after purchase.
- Choose items like apples, pears, peaches and sweet potatoes to try first. Avoid foods that may be stringy or hard for baby to swallow, such as green beans or peas with shells, unless you pass them through a fine strainer after they have been cooked and blended.

2. Clean and prepare the food. The next step is to prepare the food for cooking or serving -- this involves cleaning the food and removing any parts that the baby cannot chew or digest -- such as skins, pips, nuts, seeds and fat.

- Wash all fruits and vegetables thoroughly. Peel foods with skins and core items with seeds. Dice vegetables into similar sized cubes so they will cook evenly. In terms of quantity, 2 lbs. (900 g) of clean, diced produce will make around 2 cups (300 g) of homemade baby food.

- You can prepare meat and poultry by washing, removing the skin and trimming any fat before cooking. Grains like quinoa and millet should be prepared according to the instructions on the package.

3. Cook the food by steaming, boiling or baking. If you're preparing a ripe fruit -- like a soft pear or avocado -- you can simply mash it up with a fork and serve immediately. Vegetables, meat and grains on the other hand, will need to be cooked first. You have several options when it comes to cooking methods:

- Steaming is the best option when it comes to cooking vegetables, as it preserves the most nutrients. Use a steamer basket, or simply place a colander over a boiling saucepan of water. Steam produce until it is tender, usually about 10 to 15 minutes.
- Boiling can be used to cook grains, vegetables and certain animal produce. You can boil the food in a broth to add more flavor, if you wish.
- Baking is a good option for things like sweet potatoes, cruciferous veggies, meat and poultry. You can add a little flavor to these items by adding herbs and mild spices during baking (don't be afraid to give your baby flavor.)

4. When processing baby food, try to work in small batches. This ensures that the ingredients are thoroughly mixed. Also keep in mind that some foods will require the addition of a little liquid in order to achieve the correct consistency -- this liquid could be water, breast milk, formula or a little of the preserved cooking water (if the food was boiled).

5. Cool and puree the food. Once the food is thoroughly cooked, set it aside and allow it cool fully. Make sure that meat and poultry products have no traces of pink left, as babies are more susceptible to food poisoning.

- Choose a processing method. Small babies will need their food pureed into a creamy texture before eating, whereas older babies can handle chunkier foods. The method you choose to process your baby food will depend on the age of the baby and your own personal preferences.
- Some parents choose to invest in fancy all-in-one baby food makers, which can cook, puree, defrost and reheat fruit, vegetables and meat. These are a little on the pricey side, but make making your own baby food a breeze.
- Alternatively, you can use your regular kitchen blender, food processor or hand-held blender to process food into a smooth puree. These are fast and easy to use (and eliminate the need to buy another gadget) but may be a pain to assemble, clean and dismantle if you're only working with small quantities of food.
- You could also try using a try using a hand-turned food mill or a baby food grinder. Both of these gadget are non-electric and portable. These work well and are relatively inexpensive, but are slower require more physical effort to operate.
- Lastly, for very soft produce like ripe bananas, avocados and baked sweet potatoes, you can simply use a good old-fashioned fork to mash the food into the desired consistency.

6. Serve or store the food. Once your homemade baby food is cooked, cooled and pureed, you can

serve some of it immediately, then store the rest for later use. It's very important to store homemade baby food correctly, so it doesn't spoil or develop bacteria that will make your baby ill.

- Spoon the baby food into food safe glass jars or plastic containers with airtight lids and place in the refrigerator. Label the container with the date the food was made, so you can keep track of freshness and dispose of any foods that are more than 3 days old.
- Alternatively, you can spoon the food into covered ice cube trays and freeze. Once the cubes have frozen fully, remove them from the tray and place in a sealable plastic bag. Each cube of baby food will be enough for one portion, so defrost accordingly.
- You can thaw frozen baby food by placing it in the refrigerator overnight, or by setting the container or bag containing the food in a pan of warm water (not over direct heat) for approximately 20 minutes.
- Frozen pureed fruit and vegetables will keep for 6 to 8 months, while frozen meat and poultry will stay fresh for between one and two months.
- As making your own baby food can be pretty labor-intensive, a good strategy is to make large quantities of baby food on a single day, then freeze it for later use.

## Part 2

### Experimenting with Different Foods

1. Start with traditional baby foods. Most traditional baby food is comprised of soft, naturally sweet fruits and vegetables that are easy to prepare.

- Such foods include fruit like bananas, pears, blueberries, peaches, apricots, prunes, mangoes and apples and vegetables like sweet potatoes, butternut squash, sweet peppers, avocado, carrots and peas.
- These foods are popular as they are easy to prepare and enjoyed by most babies. They are a good place to start when you first introduce your baby to solids, but don't be afraid to branch out and try more adventures foods.
- This will help to expand your baby's taste buds and make mealtimes more interesting. Be

careful not to overwhelm your baby however -- try introducing one new food at a time and wait at least three days before introducing another. This will help you to easily identify the cause of any allergic reactions.

2. Experiment with stewed meats. Stewed meats are a great first food for babies -- they are tasty, nutritious and can be enjoyed by the rest of the family as well, which is always a bonus.

- Try making a beef stew using some light Chinese or Mexican flavors, such as soy sauce or mild poblano chillies (yes, chillies!). Babies from around the world are commonly introduced to these more intense flavors from a very early age.

- Alternatively, you could try cooking a pork shoulder with some citrus juice for a tasty dinner that will keep baby and the rest of the family happy.

3. Feed your baby fish. Traditionally, parents were advised to avoid feeding their baby fish and other potentially allergenic foods until they were at least a year old. Thinking on this subject, however, has recently changed.

- A study published in 2008 by the American Academy of Pediatrics stated that it's safe to feed these foods to babies over the age of 6 months, provided they show no signs of allergies (food or otherwise), don't suffer from asthma and have no family history of either.

- Therefore, you should consider feeding your baby fish like salmon, which is full of healthy fats and is highly nutritious. Try simmering the salmon in a pot of lightly seasoned water until it's fully cooked. Allow it to cool before pureeing (for younger babies), mashing into a bowl of carrots or other vegetables, or simply breaking it up into small chunks (for older babies).

4. Give your baby whole grains. It's a good idea to start your baby on whole grains such as quinoa and millet as early as possible.

- Whole grains introduce your baby to a whole new world of texture and encourages them to use their mouth and tongue in more advanced ways, which can help them with their speech later on.
- Whole grains don't need to be bland and boring, you can spice them up by cooking them in chicken or vegetable stock, or by mixing them with soft, flavorsome veggies like onions or butternut squash.

5. Try eggs. Like with fish, parents were traditionally were advised to avoid feeding their babies eggs until they were a year old. Nowadays, it's believed that babies can eat eggs from the start, provided they show no signs of allergies or have no family history of allergies.

- Eggs are very nutritious, containing high levels of proteins, B vitamins and other important minerals. You can cook them anyway you like -- scrambled, poached, fried or cooked into an omelette.
- Just make sure that both the white and yolk are cooked until solid -- undercooked or lightly cooked eggs can cause food poisoning.

- Try mashing a hard boiled egg with half an avocado, mixing scrambled egg with some vegetable puree, or adding a chopped fried egg to rice or oatmeal (for older babies).

6. Experiment with herbs and mild spices. Many parents become stuck on the notion that baby food needs to be bland and tasteless -- but this is not the case at all! Babies are fully capable of enjoying a wide variety of flavors.

- Try adding some rosemary to the pan when you're roasting butternut squash for pureeing, sprinkle some cumin or garlic powder on a cooked chicken breast, add a dash of cinnamon to your baby's oatmeal, or add a little chopped parsley to mashed potatoes.
- Babies can also tolerate spicy foods much better than you might think. Of course, you don't want to burn or irritate your babies mouth, but you can certainly think about adding some pureed peppers (mild varieties like Anaheims and poblanos) to things like vegetable purees and meat stews.

7. Try sour fruits. It may come as a surprise to learn that many babies enjoy the taste of sour foods. You can find out if your baby is one of them by pureeing some pitted sour cherries. You could also try stewed, unsweetened rhubarb or pureed plums, both of which have a tart, refreshing flavor.

## Part 3

### Introducing your Baby to Solids

1. Be careful with temperature. Solid baby food should be served no hotter than body temperature, to avoid burning the baby's mouth.

- You should be especially careful when reheating pre-prepared foods in the microwave, as the microwave can reheat food unevenly, creating hotspots in certain areas.
- Therefore, when you remove food from the microwave, give it a good stir to distribute the heat evenly, then leave it to sit for a few minutes until reaches room temperature.

2. Don't keep leftovers. When feeding your baby, try to measure out exact portions for each meal. This helps to avoid waste, as you won't be able to save any leftovers. This is due to the high chance that your baby's saliva will get into the food as you spoon feed him/her, which makes it much easier for bacteria to grow in the food.

3. Don't sweeten your baby's food. You should never sweeten your baby's food before feeding.

Babies don't require any extra sugar, especially given the high rates of childhood obesity nowadays. You shouldn't use any alternative sweeteners like corn syrup or honey either, as these can cause a potentially fatal form of food poisoning in babies known as botulism.

4. Avoid exposing your baby to nitrates. Nitrates are chemicals found in water and soil which can cause a certain type of anemia (known as methemoglobinemia) in exposed babies. These nitrates are eliminated from all store-bought baby foods, but can be a problem in homemade versions (especially if you use well water).

- As the major source of nitrates in baby foods comes from the use of well water, it's a good idea to have your well tested to ensure that the water contains less than 10ppm of nitrates.
- The level of nitrates increases in unfrozen food over time, so use fresh fruits and vegetables within a couple of days of purchase, freeze pre-prepared baby food as soon after cooking as possible and consider using frozen packets of veggies like beets, carrots, green beans, spinach, and squash (instead of fresh versions) as these tend to have the highest level of nitrates.

5. Feed your baby the same food as the rest of the family. Instead of preparing separate meals for your baby, make life easier for yourself by grinding, mashing or pureeing the same meal that the rest of your family is eating.

- This saves you time and effort, but will also help to train your baby to eat the same food as everyone else, which can come in handy as your baby grows up.
- Babies can eat most healthy foods that the rest of the family eats, provided they are mashed up or blended to the correct consistency -- stews, soups and casseroles can all be adapted to become baby appropriate.

## How to make Healthy Baby Food

Save some money on baby food--make your own! Healthy, tasty baby food can be had for far less than you would have paid in the grocery store. It's not that difficult! Plus, you can enjoy knowing exactly what food goes into your baby.

### Ingredients

#### Pumpkin Puree Baby Food

- 1 sugar pumpkin
- Water
- A pinch of cinnamon and/or nutmeg.

#### Banana-Cado Baby Food

- Ripe avocado
- 1 Banana

### Steps

1. Find small containers to store the food. Sterilize your containers in the dishwasher or sterilizer.

2. Buy fresh fruit or vegetables that are at the peak of ripeness. You can also use frozen food if you'd

like, which can be fresher if the fruit/vegetable is out of season. Look at the ingredients of frozen portions carefully to avoid any additives like sugar or salt.

3. Clean the fruit/veggie carefully and remove any rotting spots. Peel the fruit. Steam the veggies or cook them in the microwave in a bit of water. Follow the directions and make sure the food is soft. It is not necessary to cook the fruit.

4. Chop the food in a food processor until it is very smooth. Add warm water if necessary until you get a smooth consistency.

5. Pour a single serving size into each container and freeze immediately.

## Method 1

### Pumpkin Puree Baby Food

1. Cut the pumpkin in half. Remove all the seeds, taking care not to miss any.

2. Place each half face down in a baking pan. Cover with 1 to 2 inches (2.5 to 5.1 cm) of water.

3. Bake at 400°F for 40 minutes to 1 hour. Take the pumpkin out of the oven when the skin is wrinkled and the pumpkin is soft when pressed.

4. Scrape out the insides. Mash or puree until smooth and free of chunks. Remove any seeds you may have missed.

## Method 2

### Banana-Cado Baby Food

1. Peel the avocado. Take the pit out. Then, use a fork to mash into a paste.

2. Peel the banana. Use a fork to mash into a paste.

3. Combine the pastes in a food processor. Puree until mixture is smooth and free of chunks.

## How to Choose Healthy Snacks for your Toddler

There are a wide variety of healthy snacks you can serve to your toddler. However, there are many unhealthy choices that parents commonly provide to their children. Not only can these unhealthy snacks cause health problems, but they create the foundation for poor dietary decisions later in life. Ultimately, by focusing on fruits and vegetables, creating a balanced snack routine, avoiding unhealthy foods, and learning about specific healthy snacks you can create, you'll be better equipped to choose healthy snacks for your toddler.

### Part 1

#### Focusing on Fruits and Vegetables

1. Serve fruit. Fruit is one of the best snacks you can provide your toddler. Not only does fruit

contain many vitamins that your toddler needs to grow healthy, but they contain fiber. Ultimately, by serving your toddler fruit, you'll be creating the foundation of healthy nutrition habits for the rest of their life.

- Provide fresh fruits like apples, peaches, pears, bananas, grapes, strawberries, and oranges.
- Give them dried fruits like apples, apricots, peaches, raisins, and cranberries.
- Make sure to slice fruit thinly, pit fruit that needs to be pitted, and remove other potential dangers.
- A snack of fruit should consist of about 75 calories. This will typically translate to about one cup of berries or one small fruit (like a banana, pear, or apple).

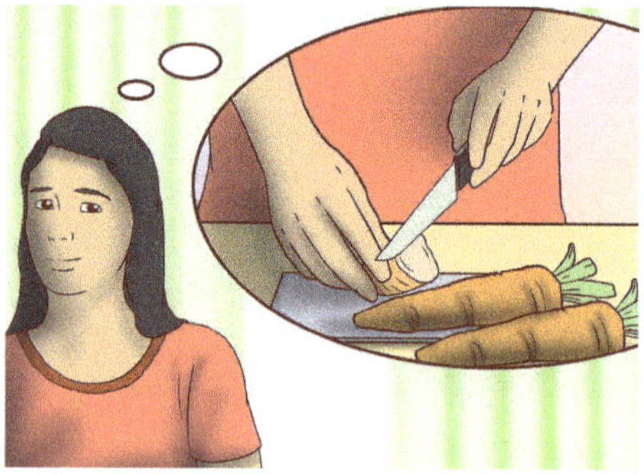

2. Provide fresh vegetables. Like fruit, vegetables are one of the best healthy snacks for your toddler. By providing them vegetables for snacks, you'll be helping your toddler get the vitamins they need and you'll create the foundation for healthy eating habits.

- Give them vegetables like carrots, green beans, cauliflower, broccoli, spinach, or avocado slices.
- Feel free to cook or steam vegetables. Avoid using butter or oil to cook them.
- Vegetables should be thinly sliced or should be bite sized.
- A snack of vegetables for a 2-year-old should be about 2 tablespoons for most vegetables. However, toddlers can eat more of some vegetables, like celery or tomatoes. For example, you may serve your toddler half a dozen three to four inch pieces of celery or one or two small tomatoes.

3. Allow your toddler to choose. When it comes to serving fruits and vegetables to your toddler,

you should allow them the ability to pick what they want to eat. This is important, as you want to promote independence and give your child the ability to develop their own tastes. Ultimately, if they're choosing a fruit or vegetable, they'll be picking something healthy.

- Give your toddler the choice between two or three types of fruits or vegetables. For instance, if you're serving vegetables as a snack, ask if they want broccoli, tomatoes, or cucumbers.
- Don't always give them the same choices. Rotate what you offer, so your toddler winds up choosing different vegetables.

## Part 2

### Creating a Balanced Snack Routine

1. Establish a snack plan. By creating a snack plan, you'll have an idea of what healthy snacks you'll give to your toddler over the course of a week. Thus, you'll be able to make sure you have all the ingredients you need.

- Plan to provide three snacks every day, in addition to three meals. This way, your toddler will be eating something every three or three hours.
- Vary your snacks throughout the day. If you provide a dairy-heavy snack in the morning, focus on vegetables on fruits in the afternoon.
- Map out your snacks for the entire week. For instance, sit down at the beginning of the week and plan all your snacks.

2. Include whole grains. Whole grains an important part of creating a balanced snack menu for

your toddler. They are also a great source of fiber for toddlers and adults alike. Thus, you should focus on whole grains when providing your toddler with snacks. Remember:

- To think about whole grain crackers and similar snacks. Rice cakes are another good snack.
- To use whole wheat bread when making any sort of snack.
- To look for whole grain cereals free from added sugar (or with very little added sugar).

3. Provide only quality dairy products. Snacks that include dairy are important because they contain calcium, iron, and other important vitamins. Thus, you need to make sure you include dairy products in your snack plan.

- Your child should have three servings of dairy a day. When it comes to processed cheese, this equates to 1 slice, 1 mini string cheese, and 1 mini baby bell. Feel free to include these in your toddler's snacks.
- One small pot (about 125 ml) of yogurt makes for a great snack. At the same time, you can serve half of a small pot of yogurt with fruit or vegetables.
- Consider providing your child with a 3 or 4 ounce cup (100 to 120 ml) of milk with their snack. Use semi skimmed milk for toddlers over 2 years old. Those under 2 years old should be served 3 ounces (100 ml) or less of whole milk.

4. Limit meat intake. Like dairy, meat is an important source of iron and other vitamins that toddlers need. As a result, make sure to include meat in their snack rotation. However, you should also limit the amount of meat and type of meat your toddler consumes.

- Focus on lean meats like fish, good cuts of beef or pork, or chicken and turkey.
- Avoid processed meat, if you can. This includes many types of lunch meats like salami, bologna, some types of ham, and pepperoni. When shopping for lunch or deli meat, look for meats that do not include nitrates or nitrites.
- The total amount of meat a 2-year-old should consume per day is 2 ounces. Toddlers that are three years old can eat 3 to 4 ounces (85 to 113 grams) of meat. Make sure you account for your toddler's daily consumption when serving them meat for snacks.
- Provide ½ to 1 egg (poached, boiled, or fried) as an alternative to meat.

## Part 3

### Avoiding Unhealthy Foods

1. Moderate consumption of fruit juice. Despite the claims of some fruit juice makers, drinking a lot of fruit juice can hurt a toddler's health. Ultimately, fruit juice contains a lot of sugar, and should be limited.

- Avoid juices with added sugar.
- Juices advertised as 100% fruit juice still have a lot of sugar – often equal to the sugar and/or calories contained in a soda.
- Toddlers should drink no more than 4 ounces (120 millimeters) of fruit juice per day.

2. Stay away from snacks with added sugar. Snacks with added sugar are one of the worst things

you can give your toddler. Not only are they unhealthy, but they help establish bad eating habits. If your toddler gets used to eating foods with added sugar, they'll continue that habit into adulthood.

- Avoid cereals with added sugar, like Frosted Flakes.
- Snacks high in sugar could aggravate conditions like juvenile diabetes.
- It is okay for your toddler to have things like birthday cake, ice cream, or similar snacks as a treat. However, don't establish it as a habit.

3. Limit consumption of foods high in saturated fat. Not only are these foods unhealthy over the long run, but they can cause digestive problems like diarrhea. Avoid:

- Fried food. For example, mini corn dogs are not a good snack for your toddler.
- An excessive amount of cheese.
- Fatty cuts of meat. Limit consumption of sausages and some cuts of beef or pork.

## Part 4

### Creating Healthy Snacks

1. Offer apple slices with peanut butter. By combining two simple things together, you'll create a tasty snack that your toddler might get really excited about. When preparing the snack:

- Use peanut butter with no added oils. Natural peanut butter will only contain peanuts and salt.
- Serve a quarter to a third of a small apple to your toddler along with a quarter or half of a tablespoon of peanut butter – the amount varies with age.
- Make sure you slice the apple thinly, so your toddler can eat it easily.
- If food allergies run in your family, consult your pediatrician before serving peanut butter to a toddler for the first time.

2. Provide cottage cheese and peach slices. Whether a toddler or an adult, many people enjoy the combination of cottage cheese and peaches. In the end, this is a simple, healthy, and delicious snack that your toddler may love.

- Set aside no more than a quarter cup of canned peaches. Make sure the peaches have been canned in their own juices.
- Add no more than 1 or 2 tablespoons of cottage cheese on top of the peaches.

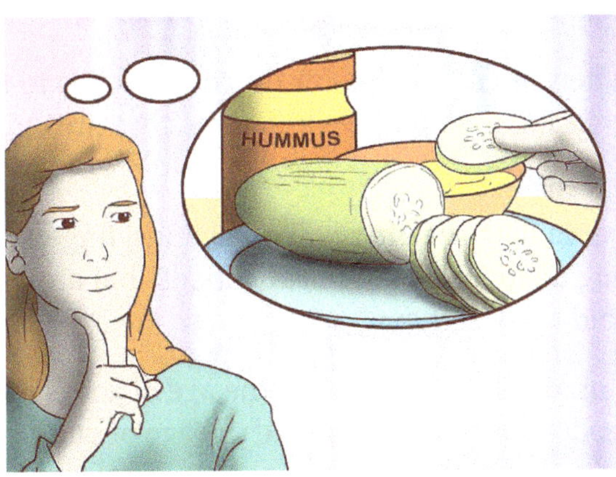


3. Serve cucumbers with hummus. Cucumbers and hummus are a healthy combination that your toddler may get excited about. When eating cucumbers and hummus, your toddler will not only get vitamins from the cucumber, but protein from the hummus.

- Thinly slice 1/4th of a medium cucumber and place them on a plate.

- Portion out 1 or 2 tablespoons of hummus next to the cucumber.
- Consider substituting hummus for low fat salad dressing.
- Think about substituting cucumbers for red peppers or a similar vegetable.

## How to Serve Healthy and Appealing Toddler Snacks

If you have a toddler, feeding them a healthy and nutritious snack may not be the easiest task. Toddlers are notorious for being picky eaters. In addition, one day they may love something and the next day they decide they hate it. That's why it's important to try make healthy and nutritious foods appealing to toddlers. If they're enticed to try a food, they're more likely to enjoy it and continue to like it. Try serving kid-friendly foods to your toddler that are not only nutritious, but also appealing to them. They'll be eating nutrient-dense snack foods without complaint.

### Method 1

#### Cooking with Kid-Friendly Foods

1. Choose kid-sized foods. When you're looking for nutritious foods to feed your toddler, you need to make sure you pick appropriate foods. Choosing items that are small in size or that are "toddler-sized" will be helpful.

- Toddlers need to have smaller sized foods. Their hands, fingers, mouth and teeth are smaller than adults'. Cutting up foods or purchasing foods that are smaller in size make it easier for your toddler to hold and eat them.
- The appropriate size of foods will depend on the age of your toddler. Very small items (like halved grapes) are needed for toddlers around the age of one and two. As they get older, it's safe to allow them to have slightly larger items (like whole grapes).
- Try items like: grapes (cut in half), dry cereal, whole grain crackers, hard boiled eggs, pitted cherries or sugar snap peas.
- You can also make foods toddler-sized. Cutting up or chopping foods into bite sized pieces also works.

2. Make snacks dippable. Another great way to get toddlers to enjoy more nutritious foods is by allowing them to dip. Consider serving nutritious foods with a fun dip for your toddler.

- Toddlers get an enjoyment at having some control over how they eat their foods. If you provide them a little bowl of sauce, they get to decide how much dip to have with their foods.
- Serving foods with a dip is also a great way to get your toddler to try new foods or ones they previously didn't like. For example, if they didn't like carrots before, try serving it with hummus.
- Ideas include: fruit with a yogurt dip, whole grain pita chips with hummus, sugar snap peas and ranch dip.

3. Try sweeter foods. Part of the reason toddlers are such picky eaters is that they have more sensitive tastes. Be mindful of this and choose foods that are naturally more sweet.

- Toddlers frequently have no issues with fruit. That's because fruits naturally sweet and more palatable to toddlers.
- Vegetables can be a little bit bitter which can turn toddlers off. Stick to naturally sweet vegetables to help them expand their tastes.
- Sweeter veggies to try include: sugar snap peas, corn, sweet peppers, beets, sweet potatoes, butternut squash, pumpkin and carrots.

4. Choose softer foods. Another thing to consider when serving toddler-friendly food is the texture. If foods are too hard, it may not be a food your toddler can eat well.

- Your toddler may seem to not like certain foods, when in fact they're just having some difficulty chewing or eating them.
- Foods that are too hard to bite through or too difficult to chew won't be appealing to your toddler.
- Make sure foods are soft enough for your toddler. You may need to cook things or cut them in very small pieces in order for your toddler to enjoy.
- For example, you could blanch raw vegetables. They're usually very hard and crunchy, but once blanched are slightly softer and easier to chew.

5. Avoid foods that may be a choking hazard. "Slippery foods" (whole grapes, large pieces of meat or chicken, hot dogs, candy); small, hard foods (nuts, seeds, popcorn, chips, pretzels, raw carrots, raisins); and sticky foods (peanut butter, marshmallows) can all pose a choking hazard. You may want to avoid these foods entirely until your toddler is older, or you may just need to be extra careful with these foods, making sure you cut them to the appropriate size for a toddler.

6. Watch for allergies. The most common food allergies are milk, eggs, peanuts and other nuts, soybeans, wheat, fish, and shellfish. Most kids outgrow their food allergies, but it is important to identify them to avoid serious reactions. If your child experiences any of the following after eating,

they may be having an allergic reaction: hives; swelling; itching lips, tongue, or mouth; abdominal pain; nausea; vomiting; diarrhea; wheezing; shortness of breath; or lightheadedness.

- Some children may have a serious, possibly life-threatening allergic reaction to foods known as anaphylaxis. If they experience swelling of the airway, serious difficulty with breathing, a drop in blood pressure, or two or more of the above symptoms simultaneously, call emergency services immediately.

## Method 2

### Toddler-Friendly Snack Recipes

1. Try some quick and easy snacks. You don't always have time to prepare an elaborate snack for your toddler. There are a number of things you can keep on hand or quickly whip up that your toddler is likely to find appealing. These things include:

- Small cubes of cheese and diced apples
- Canned pineapple chunks
- Whole grain, low-sugar dry cereal
- Whole grain crackers with cottage cheese
- Plain low-fat yogurt with sliced strawberries
- Sliced banana
- Sliced avocado

2. Build fruit kebabs. A great way to get your toddler to eat a healthy snack is by getting them involved in the preparation. Fruit kebabs are a great toddler snack plus they can help make them. Note, however, that wooden skewers can present a safety hazard – make sure your child is seated when eating the kababs.

- Start by washing a few of your toddlers favorite fruits; however, if there is a fruit they don't like, this is a great recipe to use it in since it'll be paired with items they do enjoy.
- If fruits are large (like pineapples or melons), slice the fruit into 1 – 2 inch pieces.

- Thread fruits on a wooden skewers. Alternate between each different type of fruit.
- For example, put on a strawberry, followed by a small piece of pineapple, followed by half a grape and end with a pitted cherry. Serve immediately or put in the refrigerator until ready to eat.

3. Make a homemade snack mix. Another recipe that your toddler can help you make is a homemade snack mix. It's fun for them to dump ingredients in a bowl and stir together.

- Set out a variety of nutritious snacks that your toddler already enjoys.
- Hand your toddler a 1 cup measuring cup. Have them scoop up 1 cup of each of their favorite items.
- Ask them to dump each item in a large bowl. Give them a wooden spoon and allow them to stir together their snack mix. Serve your toddler a 1/2 cup portion.

4. Serve fruit nachos. A unique and very toddler-friendly snack are fruit nachos. Your toddler will be able to help you make these and enjoy them.

- Start by slicing an apple and a pear into 1/4 inch thin slices. These will be your chips. Layer them on a plate or baking sheet in flat layers.
- Melt 1/2 cup of semisweet chocolate chips in a microwave in a small bowl. In a separate bowl, heat up about 1/2 cup of peanut or almond butter. Stir each until they're slightly fluid.

- Dip a spoon into each the chocolate and peanut butter. Have your toddler drizzle the chocolate and peanut butter over the apple and pear slices.
- Then, have them sprinkle on 1/2 cup of unsweetened shredded coconut and a dusting of cinnamon. Serve immediately.

5. Make kid-friendly "sushi." Although traditional sushi is not a toddler-friendly food (young children should never eat raw or under-cooked fish), you can make a look-alike version of this finger food at home using toddler-friendly foods. They'll be excited to enjoy this unique food.

- Start by laying out a 12" whole wheat tortilla. Spread on 2 tablespoons of garden vegetable cream cheese in an even layer.
- Then layer out two to three slices of turkey or ham deli meat and one to two slices of their favorite cheese. On top of the cheese, arrange a single layer of baby spinach leaves.
- Roll the tortilla up like a jelly roll or a sushi roll. Wrap tightly in plastic wrap and refrigerator for 30 – 60 minutes.
- Take the "sushi" out of the refrigerator and slice in 2" rounds. Serve immediately.

## Method 3

### Encouraging your Child to Eat Nutritious Foods

1. Lead by example. If you want your toddler to eat more nutritious foods, the first thing you need to do is lead by example. If you're not eating well, your toddler may not either.

- You may be surprised how much your toddler is learning from you. But at this age, they're mimicking their parents behaviors a lot.
- Toddlers are watching what you eat, how you eat and how you're talking about different foods.
- Talk positively about healthy foods and let them see you having healthy and nutritious foods at meals and snacks.

2. Let your child pick out nutritious foods. One great way to get your child interested in healthier foods is by letting them help choose their foods. Consider bringing your child along to the grocery store with you. Let them get involved in picking some of the foods they will eat.

- Talk about healthy foods and finding foods to have as snacks. Stroll through the produce section and ask what they would like to have as a snack.
- For example, as you're passing by the fruit, mention how much your toddler loves fruit and how it'd be a great snack. Then ask them to pick something out to eat that week or day.
- Also, try to stay out of "trouble aisles." If your child loves chips or cookies, stay away from the aisles that have them. If they're not looking at it or see it, they may not ask for it.

3. Get your child involved in cooking. In addition to letting your toddler participate in the shopping, let them get involved in some food preparation.

- Studies have shown that if you allow your kids to get involved in the cooking or preparation of meals or snacks, they're more likely to eat them.
- When it's time for a snack or your toddler mentions they're hungry, ask them if they'd like to help you make their snack.
- Make sure to choose tasks that are toddler-friendly. They can stir, roll out or help measure different foods.

4. Be patient. With all things, it pays to be patient with your toddler. They may not like a certain food initially or be reluctant to try it. But be patient and take your time as they grow and expand their palates.

- Studies have shown that it can take a toddler 15 – 30 tries of a food item before they begin to learn to like it.
- This is especially true with some vegetables and whole grains that have a slightly bitter or unique flavor or texture.
- They key to getting your child to eat healthy snacks, is to keep presenting healthy foods over and over again. In time, they will become used to and accustomed to these foods.

## How to make Vegetables more Appealing to Kids

Have you ever tried to offer your kids fruit and vegetables, and they just say no? By choosing kid-friendly vegetables, cooking simply, and disguising vegetables, you can help your kids get the nutrition they need.

### Method 1

#### Starting with Kid-Friendly Vegetables

1. Choose sweeter vegetables. Vegetables like carrots, peas and sweet potatoes offer a sweeter flavor than many of the vegetables children sometimes refuse to touch (like broccoli and brussels sprouts). As children are genetically driven to eat sweeter foods, it makes sense to start with the sweetest vegetables. You can even make them sweeter by adding a honey glaze for carrots, or maple syrup and brown sugar for sweet potatoes.

2. Choose non-leafy vegetables. Children are also genetically driven to avoid the veggies that look the most like leafy plants. Cutting, dicing, and blending can help disguise the leafiness, but starting with butternut squash or sweet peas may help get the ball rolling.

3 .Introduce bitter vegetables slowly. Many people have a higher sensitivity to bitterness than others. This is especially true in children, and this sensitivity tends to decrease with age. So, by starting kids with kid-friendly vegetables, and slowly introducing the more difficult ones can get the child interested (especially if you make it a point to show them your enjoyment of the vegetables).

## Method 2

### Cooking Simply

1. Don't mix a ton of vegetables together in a single dish. Starting simply by having no more than one or two veggies in a single dish will make the veggies more appealing. Slowly introduce dishes that are more complex. For instance, if you know that your child likes broccoli, you can mix it with

a smooth pasta sauce and pasta to make a more balanced meal. Don't try adding roasted peppers if you know your child doesn't like it. The sauce may not completely cover the taste or texture.

2. Use only completely disguised/blended veggies in soft or liquid dishes. While disguising vegetables can be a real solution, be careful not to hide crunchy, flavorful vegetables that a kid professes a dislike to in a soft dish like stuffing. While they may be perfectly willing to eat the stuffing, for instance, chomping down on an onion may make them pause before eating the dish again. The same thing goes with sauces and salsa. Any professed dislike for a vegetable due to texture that is not properly blended will likely cause a similar reaction to eating the vegetable alone.

3. Add veggies with unusual textures slowly. Kids are more sensitive to textures in foods than adults. Whether it's sliminess or a "wet-crunch," kids (and adults) can be sensitive to food textures. Going with soft, but not slimy, or pleasantly crisp vegetables (like carrots), can make eating vegetables fun for kids.

4. Add a simple flavor enhancer that kids love. Adding lemon juice or cheese to broccoli can help

make the veggies more appealing. Honey or maple syrup can make cooked carrots more appetizing. In any case, they will be more likely to try veggies topped with flavors they love.

- Dips can be a great way to get kids to eat fresh crunchy veggies such as carrots or celery. Ranch dressing works especially well. Plain hummus can also make a great dip that is both kid-friendly and nutritious.
- Peanut butter is also useful in getting kids to eat more veggies. Carrots and peanut butter can be a tasty treat.

## Method 3

### Disguising Vegetables

1. Bake a vegetable-based bread. Not only is this tasty, if you use fresh vegetables, it's packing a nutritious punch. If your recipe is too-carb heavy, this might need to be an occasional, rather than regular, snack. However, sweet potato bread is a great way for kids to get a lot of needed nutrients.

2. Make a sweet, but vegetable-containing smoothie. With the right proportions, you can use this to include some of the trickier vegetables in your kids' diets. Spinach and kale are pretty easy to include. It's important to have enough sweet fruits or honey to balance the bitterness of the greens. However, it will be harder to mask veggies with strong flavors such as onions and garlic.

3. Cook a completely blended soup. A lot of kids struggle with texture as well as flavor. By blending veggies that kids normally don't like because of texture, you can incorporate it with flavors the kid does like. Sometimes it's only the texture that's the problem, and so kids will often eat the vegetable in another form that they won't touch its raw or unblended form.

4. Buy products that do the disguising for you. From smoothies to chips to popcorn and pasta, companies are trying to make traditional snacks healthier. While products that rely on processed or dehydrated vegetables shouldn't replace fresh vegetables, they can help augment veggie-poor diets. You can even try vegan versions of typically meat or dairy type products, as they often contain a lot of vegetables (check the label, though, because many of these products contain a lot of corn or soy).

- If you're struggling to get your kids to eat vegetables, your kids might like veggie burgers. Veggies burgers are often made from rice, black beans, and other healthy vegetables. Check the label to make sure.
- Your kids might enjoy fruit and veggie juices, or juice that contains both fruit and vegetables. Check the label to make sure the sugar content is not too high before implementing it regularly into your kids' diets.
- Many chip companies are now producing chips made with other vegetables than potatoes, including broccoli, beans and carrots. These chips are often quite tasty and can be paired with a nutritious veggie dip. Again, check the label to make sure the chips live up to their claims.

5. Include vegetables subtly in a recipe kids like. With meat and cheese dishes it can be easy to slip a vegetable into the mix and the kids be none-the-wiser. For instance, if you're making a home-made pasta sauce, you can blend vegetables in with the tomatoes. Then your kids will enjoy the pasta and get the vitamins and minerals they need.

6. Make the vegetable look like something else. Sometimes, simply making the veggie look like some other yummy snack can make it more appealing. Whether you disguise cauliflower as mashed potatoes or root vegetables as fries, kids will likely find these versions more appealing than in other forms. And you may find a yummier alternative for yourself as well.

## Method 4

### Getting the Kids Involved in Adding More Veggies

1. Grow a veggie garden with the kids. Growing a garden together can add physical activity as well

as a feeling of investment in the vegetables your kids eat. Choose veggies you know they like, or have them pick out seeds or plants. With time and encouragement, kids may grow to like even more vegetables, as well as to appreciate the time growing, picking, and preparing the vegetables from your garden.

- Some easy-to-grow veggies include peas, potatoes, and cabbage.

2. Bring the kids grocery shopping with you. Even if you don't have time for a garden, you can bring your kids to the grocery store. Let them pick out one or two vegetables that they think they will like. This will make your kids feel like they have some choice in the foods that get prepared at home.

3. Cook veggies with the kids. Cooking can make kids more invested in trying veggies, especially if they get to pick the recipes. Try to have several colorful cookbooks on hand with loads of easy veggie recipes. That way the kids will feel like they have lots of choices for healthy vegetable recipes they may like.

4. Keep trying. Although it may seem difficult to get kids to eat enough veggies, it's okay to keep

trying. It may take 15-20 tries before a child will accept a new food. Don't worry if the progress is slow, or they only like a couple of veggies at first. Each vegetable added is a triumph, and with encouragement, they become a healthy eater as well.

## How to get Toddlers to Eat Vegetables

Toddlers are known for refusing vegetables. Some people say that their taste buds rebel against anything that is slightly bitter. But most toddlers will learn to like a variety of vegetables, if given a chance. Here are some things you can try:

### Steps

1. Relax. Toddlers can get all the vitamins and minerals they need from other foods besides vegetable. Healthy toddlers offered a variety of foods will choose a balanced diet over time.

2. Offer healthy foods, including snack times. Toddlers have small stomachs. If their tummies are full of pretzels or fruit juice, they won't have room for vegetables at dinner time.

3. Steam vegetables with a little oil, and spices or herbs. Steaming preserves the natural flavor of the vegetable, and preserves the nutrients too.

4. Keep offering. Children can be resistant to new things, so don't worry if they reject peas at first. It can take ten or more offers before they accept a new food.

5. Don't mush it. Toddlers like to serve themselves, not be fed with a spoon. Also, putting several foods on their plate means they can choose what they feel like at the moment.

6. Relax even more. Parents often have unrealistic expectations about how much their toddlers actually need. If the child is growing well and meeting developmental milestones, he's probably fine.

7. Don't overdo it on the vegetables. Vegetables are low in calories, so kids don't want to fill up their stomachs with them. Kids are smart, and won't choose vegetables over carbohydrates if they are really hungry.

8. Serve fresh and cooked vegetables at every meal, and invite your toddler to the family dinner table.

9. Think of interesting ways to involve vegetables in your toddler's meals. If your child likes pigs-in-a-blanket, make vegetables in croissant rolls.

## How to get Kids to Try New Foods

For most parents, finding ways to encourage their picky eaters to try to enjoy new foods is a top priority. In fact, a recent survey showed more than 68 percent of registered dietitians who counsel new parents frequently receive questions about getting finicky eaters to eat at mealtime. And now, faced with a new school year, busy parents need more help than ever to ensure a nutritious, fast and convenient solution.

To help parents conquer mealtime battles, Tyson Foods and Robin Miller, author and Food Network host of Quick Fix Meals, offer the following "nuggets" of mealtime wisdom and finger food suggestions to help provide balanced nutrition and please even the pickiest of eaters:

### Steps

1. Serve more hands-on food: Let's face it—kids prefer to eat with their hands. Finger foods make ideal meals for kids since you can combine a variety of small portions on one plate. Try partnering protein-packed Tyson® 100% All Natural Chicken Nuggets with vitamin-rich green beans and complex carbohydrate-rich pasta for a mouth-watering, nutritious meal that's easy to eat with little hands. What looks like fun to your child is a well-balanced meal that you can feel good about serving.

- Muffin Tin Meals: Set up a "finger food buffet" and have your kids pick the items they'd like eat. Start with a muffin tin (or any small container with compartments) and customize the meal by filling the sections with bite-size portions of colorful, nutritious foods. Some great food ideas include: cubed cheese, whole grain cereals, grapes, sugar snap peas, baby carrots, and cherry tomatoes. Once you've filled the compartments, let them pick their items, allowing them to be hands-on with their meal.

2. Give fun, creative names to everyday nutritious foods. According to a 2009 Cornell University study, when kids were offered "X-ray vision carrots" instead of plain carrots, they ate 62 percent more carrots . Try adopting this approach in your own house by giving silly names to a variety of foods, such as "cloud fluff" for mashed potatoes or "cheese in the trees" for broccoli florets topped with cheese.

3. Provide dipping sauces. At mealtime, fill bowls with dipping sauces (i.e ranch dressing, ketchup, or honey) and put them in the middle of the table or give them to your child.

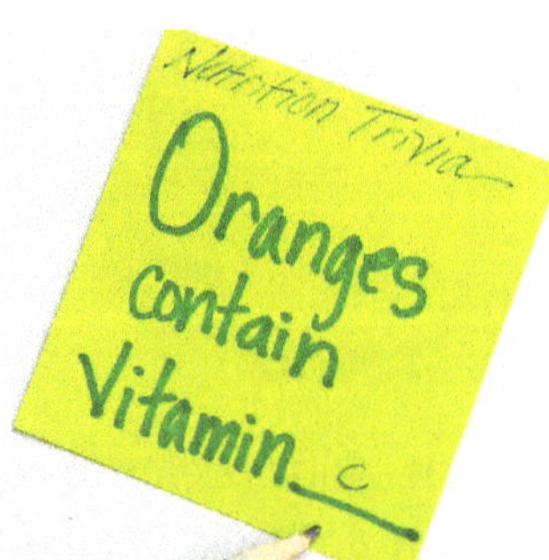


4. Play "nutrition school". Make if fun and educational for kids to learn about nutrition by asking them to figure out how many pieces of fruit or veggies make up a serving. Show them the label, and then have "lunch time" once they have figured out how much they need to eat.

5. Grow your own food. Children love running outside to check on what's growing, and they're more likely to eat something if they have grown it/watched it grow.

## How to feed a Baby or Infant Solid Food

Baby's growing up, and is ready for solid baby food! But are you prepared? Do you suddenly find yourself face-to-face with your first babysitting experience feeding a baby? Here is some help!

### Part 1

#### Knowing when Baby is Ready

1. Start when baby is ready. It is generally recommended that babies consume only formula or breast milk until about four to six months. Don't press solid food too early, as it has been linked to food allergies and even eating disorders. It can be time for solids if your baby displays the following signs:

- Baby is able to sit by his or her self or can sit with some support.
- Baby's weight has doubled.
- Baby can turn his or her head away from you if you try to do something unpleasant to the face (like wiping a runny nose).
- Baby shows interest in others eating.
- Baby shows signs of hunger even after 8 oz/236 milliliters (8 fl oz) of milk.

- Baby can show signs of fullness by turning away the head or not opening the mouth, perhaps pushing away with hands.

  For absolute reassurance if you're feeling uncertain, check with your child's doctor regarding what foods to introduce and when.

## Part 2

### Setting up a Suitable Feeding Environment

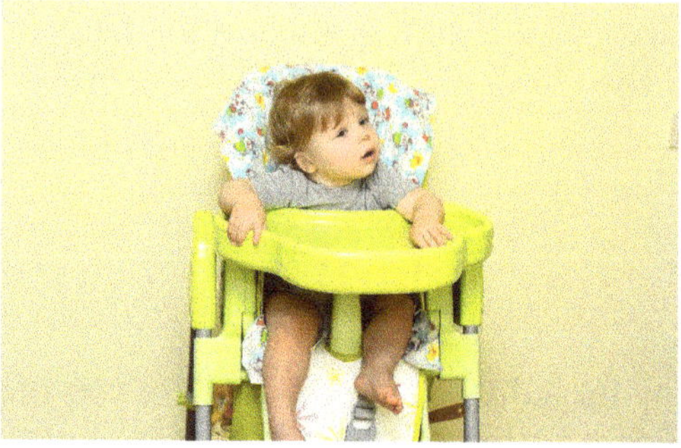

1. Use a feeding chair. A high chair is ideal, but in a pinch you can use a car seat. Have the baby sit in your lap only in desperation, because this position is awkward and will leave you messy. Be careful that the seat is set up safely and the baby secured properly.

2. Spread out a drop cloth to catch spills. Commercial messy-mats are available, but a shower curtain, a painter's drop-cloth, a garbage bag, or chair mat will also work. Or, simply be prepared to sweep and mop the floor after.

3. Get a bowl or two. You will usually need one bowl for cereal, and one for a "side dish". Generally,

choose unbreakable bowls, because babies tend to grab and drop everything. Be sure any dish used is clean and safe.

- You may wish to be careful about choosing containers made from #7 plastic due to concerns about its bisphenol A (BPA) content, which is thought to be able to leach into food and drink and may be a form of endocrine disrupter. Wide scale concern was expressed as to this type of plastic container in the late 2000s, although the research done thus far has not convinced major government food safety authorities as to its lack of safety. Since babies' immune systems are developing, many people prefer to err on the side of precaution and many products now voluntarily state that they are BPA-free. Or, you can prefer glass over plastic or simply avoid heating anything edible or drinkable in a plastic container.

4. Use a baby spoon. Regular tablespoons or dessert spoons can be hard on little baby gums. Baby spoons have a protective covering. Some are color-changing to indicate unsafe temperature. Either way, this should also be very clean.

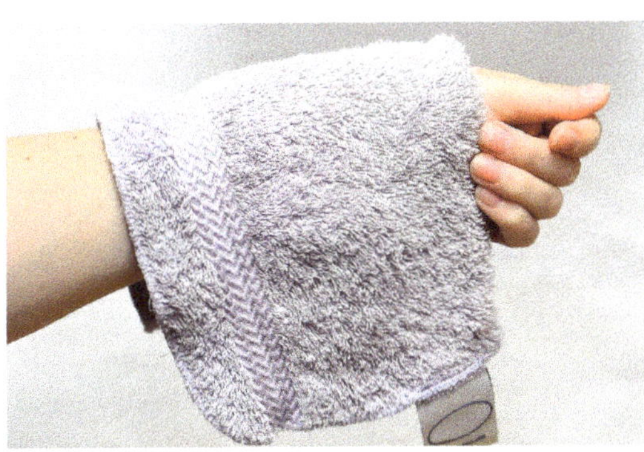

5. Have towels handy. Whether you use paper, or cloth, have some on hand. Babies get *messy*.

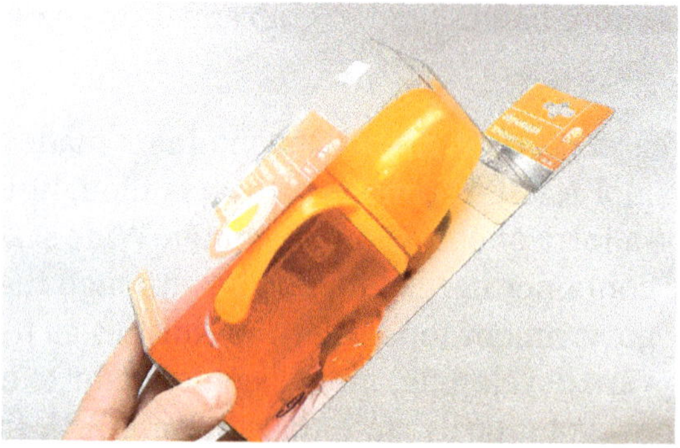

6. Use a cup. Babies on solid food need some liquid. Find out if the baby prefers using a sipper cup or a plastic cup (or you can simply make this choice for the baby). Use clean, filtered water, or juice diluted by half.

- Do not get the baby too used to juice; keep it to a minimum, as it is sugar-filled and can harm growing teeth.

## Part 3

### Choosing the First Solids

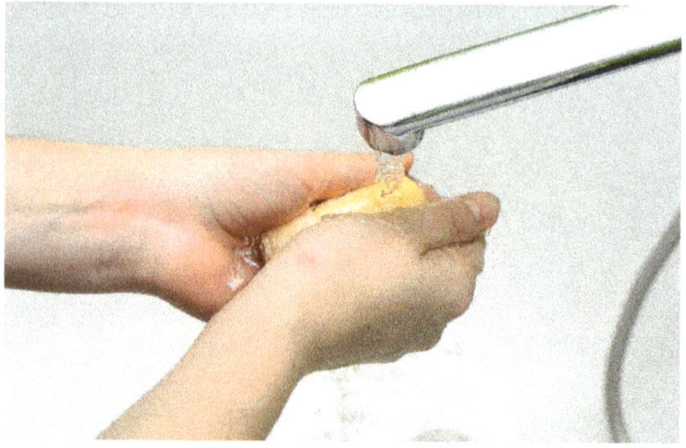

1. Wash your hands. Wash your hands before preparing or serving food.

2. Pick a finger food. If you have an older baby, choose an approved "finger food" like rice crackers, meat sticks, and the like. This can also be an "appetizer" as you are preparing other food.

3. Pick a cereal. Even experienced babies should have cereal at least for one meal—–it's one of *the*

most nutritious solid baby foods available. The cereal should be the central "entrée" (main part of the meal).

- Experienced babies will usually eat a variety of grains: oatmeal, barley, or rice. Prepare as per directions.
- You can add a little bit of baby food for flavor, or pureed fruit or vegetable.
- For a first-time feeding, rice cereal, mixed with formula or breast milk, is the typically recommended food.
- For the novice, be sure it is very liquid for easy swallowing.
- Always check the temperature of any warmed-up food before feeding the baby.

4. Choose baby food. Experienced babies usually will have some sort of prepared baby food. On commercial baby foods, the jar often will indicate the appropriate age level. If you choose to heat the food, be sure it is a safe temperature.

5. Avoid using contaminated or expired food. Check lids for airtight seal on unopened containers. Check expiration date for commercial foods. Rinse the container if possible. If feeding food from a jar or container, only do so if the food will not be saved. If not, pour a serving into a bowl, cover, and refrigerate the leftovers. Otherwise, the baby's saliva and dirty spoon can introduce bacteria and viruses into reused food. Use all food within 48 hours.

## Part 4

### Feeding Baby

1. Put a bib on baby. The bigger, the better. For feeding you may want to have something water-proof to prevent liquids from soaking the clothes under the bib.

2. Start feeding. An experienced hungry baby will usually open his or her mouth to indicate where to put the spoon. Take a spoonful of food, and feed baby. Wait until baby has swallowed before offering more food. A baby just starting on solids will eat only about a tablespoon, so don't expect more than a few bites.

3. Offer liquids. Every 5-10 bites, offer the cup. Bring the cup gently to lips if necessary, and give a sip or two. This is often very messy.

4. Watch for grabbing hands. Curious babies will tend to grab at everything in arm's reach, including the food bowl, spoon, cup, and even you. A baby will also delight in watching things drop (hence why you need either unbreakable utensils or a very soft landing).

5. Let baby help. Older babies can often feed themselves. Less experienced babies may hold onto the spoon or cup while you feed them. Encourage them to "help" even if it's messy as long as it is not becoming difficult to feed.

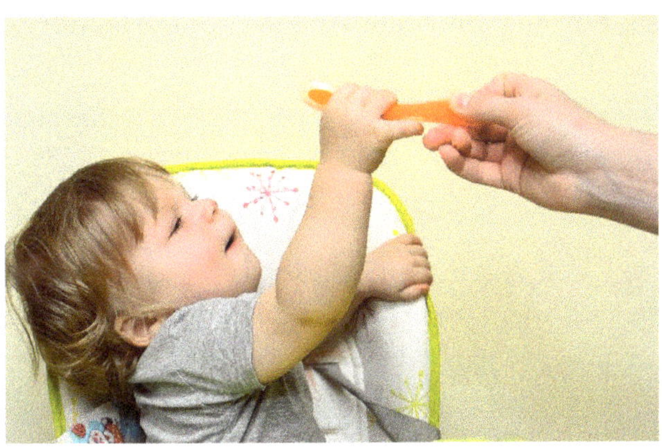

6. Know when enough is enough. If the baby is turning the head away, whimpering, crying, pushing away the spoon, or throwing food, he or she is probably done. Either remove baby from feeding area, or offer a toy or other distraction (like a clean spoon, or plastic cup or bowl) as you finish the clean-up.

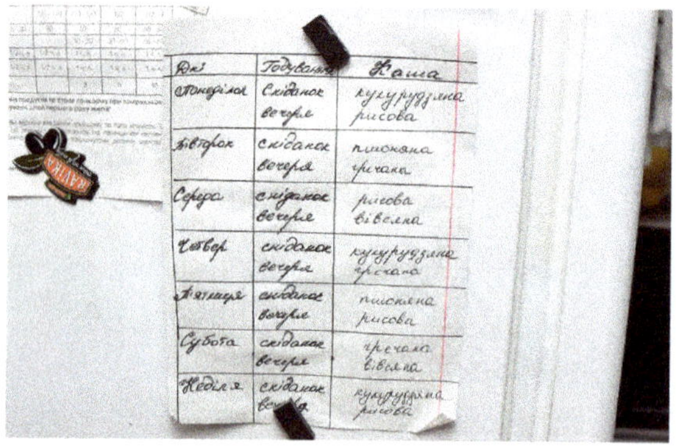

7. Record the feeding, if wished. Many parents will record what was eaten, when, and how much. A log book, calendar, or the like is useful. This is helpful for keeping an eye on possible food allergens, keeping multiple babies organized, and monitoring special dietary needs. However, it can also be just one extra task in an already very busy day of caring for your baby, so it's no biggie if you don't want to or can't find the time for it; not every person enjoys maintaining such minutiae and others simply have good memories and rely on that instead.

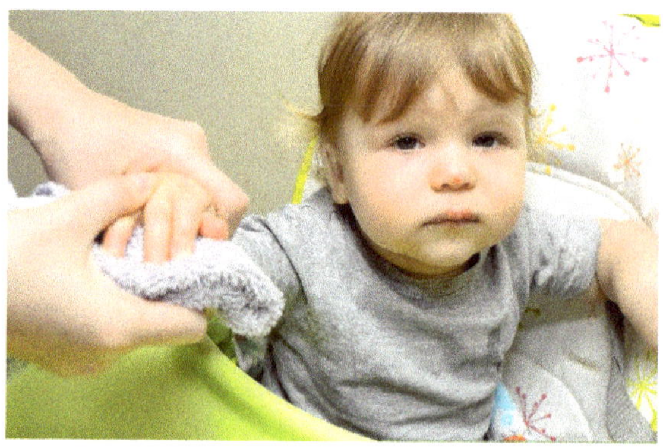

8. Clean up. Clean baby with the towels, especially face and hands. Use warm, not hot, water. Prepare dishware and containers for washing. Clean the high chair area with mild detergent and water. Prepare cloth towels, bib, and any soiled clothing for the laundry.

# Permissions

All chapters in this book are published with permission under the Creative Commons Attribution Share Alike License or equivalent. Every chapter published in this book has been scrutinized by our experts. Their significance has been extensively debated. The topics covered herein carry significant information for a comprehensive understanding. They may even be implemented as practical applications or may be referred to as a beginning point for further studies.

We would like to thank the editorial team for lending their expertise to make the book truly unique. They have played a crucial role in the development of this book. Without their invaluable contributions this book wouldn't have been possible. They have made vital efforts to compile up to date information on the varied aspects of this subject to make this book a valuable addition to the collection of many professionals and students.

This book was conceptualized with the vision of imparting up-to-date and integrated information in this field. To ensure the same, a matchless editorial board was set up. Every individual on the board went through rigorous rounds of assessment to prove their worth. After which they invested a large part of their time researching and compiling the most relevant data for our readers.

The editorial board has been involved in producing this book since its inception. They have spent rigorous hours researching and exploring the diverse topics which have resulted in the successful publishing of this book. They have passed on their knowledge of decades through this book. To expedite this challenging task, the publisher supported the team at every step. A small team of assistant editors was also appointed to further simplify the editing procedure and attain best results for the readers.

Apart from the editorial board, the designing team has also invested a significant amount of their time in understanding the subject and creating the most relevant covers. They scrutinized every image to scout for the most suitable representation of the subject and create an appropriate cover for the book.

The publishing team has been an ardent support to the editorial, designing and production team. Their endless efforts to recruit the best for this project, has resulted in the accomplishment of this book. They are a veteran in the field of academics and their pool of knowledge is as vast as their experience in printing. Their expertise and guidance has proved useful at every step. Their uncompromising quality standards have made this book an exceptional effort. Their encouragement from time to time has been an inspiration for everyone.

The publisher and the editorial board hope that this book will prove to be a valuable piece of knowledge for students, practitioners and scholars across the globe.

# Index

CPSIA information can be obtained
at www.ICGtesting.com
Printed in the USA
LVHW060854030122
707669LV00002B/158

9 781639 871056